"Jani Santamaría brings together leading Bion scholars, thinkers and practitioners to explore the dreaming dimensions of the mind. This book is a must read for all who value the aesthetic expression of the dreamwork present in any analytic encounter. Even more than that, the book highlights the dream work that exists beneath any encounter with experience."

Judy K Eekhoff, PhD FIPA, Training Supervising Psychoanalyst in Seattle, Washington, USA. She is the author of three books: *Trauma and Primitive Mental States: An Object Relations Perspective*; *Bion and Primitive Mental States: Trauma and the Symbiotic Link*; and *Bion's Emotional Links: Love, Hate, and Knowledge*.

"This book is itself a kind of dream—inviting the reader into an analytic experience where thought takes shape through the interplay of emotions and emerging meanings. Like a session in which patient and analyst co-create something new. This remarkable work is highly recommended to anyone seeking to dream new dreams."

Antonino Ferro, Pavia, member and former president of the Italian Psychoanalytic Society, member of the American Psychoanalytic Association and the International Psychoanalytical Association, author of *Psychoanalysis and Dreams: Bion, the Field and the Viscera of the Mind*.

"A book that opens the wonder of dreams and work of emotional realities in deepening life. It is a book that keeps giving us to ourselves in helpful ways. You will relish phrase after phrase, line after line and feel more of the riches that help you grow."

Michael Eigen, PhD, author of *Contact with the Depths, Faith, The Birth of Experience, Emotional Storm, The Sensitive Self, The Psychoanalytic Mystic*.

Bion, Dreamwork and the Oneiric Dimensions of the Mind

Bion, Dreamwork and the Oneiric Dimensions of the Mind allows readers to examine one of the most significant areas of clinical psychoanalytic thinking, focusing on Bion's idiom that dreaming is the central aspect of all emotional functioning and it is a full-time ongoing psychic activity.

Including chapters from leading Bionian scholars and clinicians such as Nicola Abel-Hirsch, Rudi Vermote, Anne Alvarez, Giuseppe Civitarese and Howard Levine, this book elucidates Bion's theory of the oneiric dimension and shows its importance in the development of the psychoanalytic understanding of dreams. The global cohort of contributors provides a thorough and varied exploration of dreamwork alpha, nighttime dreams, transformational dreamwork, alpha function, container/contained, and their manifestations and implications in the treatment situation, psychic development, the arts (Cezanne and Frida Kahlo) and our cultural surroundings.

This edited collection will be of interest and value to psychoanalysts and therapists of all orientations and levels of experience who want to understand dreaming and the oneiric dimensions of the mind.

Jani Santamaría Linares is Training and Supervisor Psychoanalyst of Children, Adolescents and Adults of the Mexican Psychoanalytic Association and Director of A-Santamaría Psychoanalysis Mexico A.C. She is a member of APsA, IPA and FEPAL and is co-author of *Bion Seminars at the A-Santamaria Association: Clinical and Theoretical Explorations* (2024).

The Routledge Wilfred R. Bion Studies Book Series

Series Editor:
Howard B. Levine, MD

Editorial Advisory Board:
Nicola Abel-Hirsch, Joseph Aguayo, Avner Bergstein, Lawrence J. Brown, Judith Eekhoff, Claudio Laks Eizerik, Robert D. Hinshelwood, Chris Mawson, James Ogilvie, Elias M. da Rocha Barros, Jani Santamaria, Rudi Vermote

The contributions of Wilfred Bion are among the most cited in the analytic literature. Their appeal lies not only in their content and explanatory value, but in their generative potential. Although Bion's training and many of his clinical instincts were deeply rooted in the classical tradition of Melanie Klein, his ideas have a potentially universal appeal. Rather than emphasizing a particular psychic content (e.g., Oedipal conflicts in need of resolution; splits that needed to be healed; preconceived transferences that must be allowed to form and flourish, etc.), he tried to help open and prepare the mind of the analyst (without memory, desire or theoretical preconception) for the encounter with the patient.

Bion's formulations of group mentality and the psychotic and non-psychotic portions of the mind, his theory of thinking and emphasis on facing and articulating the truth of one's existence so that one might truly learn firsthand from one's own experience, his description of psychic development (alpha function and container/contained) and his exploration of O are "non-denominational" concepts that defy relegation to a particular school or orientation of psychoanalysis. Consequently, his ideas have taken root in many places.... and those ideas continue to inform many different branches of psychoanalytic inquiry and interest.

It is with this heritage and its promise for the future developments of psychoanalysis in mind that we present *The Routledge Wilfred Bion Studies Book Series*. This series gathers together newly emerging and continually evolving contributions to psychoanalytic thinking that rest upon Bion's foundational texts and explore and extend the implications of his thought. For a full list of titles in the series, please visit the Routledge website at: https://www.routledge.com/The-Routledge-Wilfred-Bion-Studies-Book-Series/book-series/RWBSBS

Howard B. Levine, MD
Series Editor

Bion, Dreamwork and the Oneiric Dimensions of the Mind

Edited by
Jani Santamaría Linares

LONDON AND NEW YORK

First published 2026
by Routledge
4 Park Square, Milton Park, Abingdon, Oxon OX14 4RN

and by Routledge
605 Third Avenue, New York, NY 10158

Routledge is an imprint of the Taylor & Francis Group, an informa business

© 2026 selection and editorial matter, Jani Santamaría Linares; individual chapters, the contributors

The right of Jani Santamaría Linares to be identified as the author of the editorial material, and of the authors for their individual chapters, has been asserted in accordance with sections 77 and 78 of the Copyright, Designs and Patents Act 1988.

All rights reserved. No part of this book may be reprinted or reproduced or utilised in any form or by any electronic, mechanical, or other means, now known or hereafter invented, including photocopying and recording, or in any information storage or retrieval system, without permission in writing from the publishers.

Trademark notice: Product or corporate names may be trademarks or registered trademarks, and are used only for identification and explanation without intent to infringe.

Designed cover image: Wild Poppies Near Argenteuil by Claude Monet 1873

British Library Cataloguing in Publication Data
A catalogue record for this book is available from the British Library

ISBN: 978-1-032-77331-5 (hbk)
ISBN: 978-1-032-76459-7 (pbk)
ISBN: 978-1-003-48251-2 (ebk)

DOI: 10.4324/9781003482512

Typeset in Times New Roman
by Taylor & Francis Books

Contents

Dedication	x
In Memoriam	xi
Acknowledgements	xii

Introduction   1
JANI SANTAMARÍA LINARES

1   Freud's Dream and Bion's Dream   22
HOWARD B. LEVINE

2   Bion and My Patients   32
ANNE ALVAREZ

3   On Going Further to What We Know   39
NICOLA ABEL-HIRSCH

4   Dreaming, Day-dreaming and Sensing Things Together   49
PETER GOLDBERG

5   *We-ness* and Bion's Psychoanalytic Function of Intuition   61
GIUSEPPE CIVITARESE

6   "To Risk Sailing Westward to Cathay and Thence Safely Home": Oneiric States of Mind   70
AVNER BERGSTEIN

7   A Dream Is Just a Dream   84
RUDI VERMOTE

8   The Oneiric Dimensions of the Mind in the Analytic Session   90
JOÃO CARLOS BRAGA

9 Learning from Experience in the Analytic Session: Dream-
   Work-Alfa   97
   ANTONIO SAPIENZA

10 Cézanne Dreams Bion   107
   ROBERT SNELL

11 Oneiric Dimensions of the Mind in Frida Kahlo   117
   JANI SANTAMARÍA LINARES

12 Beatriz and *The Great Mystical Circus*: The Musical and Poetical
   Transformation of an Emotional Experience   136
   RAUL HARTKE AND EDU MARTINS

   Index   144

Dedication

With all my love and admiration for his infinite patience and magical way of being, I dedicate this book to my son José Luis, for being much more than a dream coming true.

My deepest gratitude to Thomas Ogden.

To José Luis González Chagoyan – my son's godfather – and Antonio Mendizabal for their pioneering work on the study of Wilfred Bion in my country, Mexico.

In Memoriam

Chris Mawson
James Gooch
Neville Symington
José Luis González Chagoyan
Antonio Sapienza
Antonio Mendizábal

Acknowledgements

I want to thank all those whose generous cooperation contributed to this book's publication and the Routledge Bion Series team for their help with manuscripts and getting the book ready.

I am grateful to the former Chairs of the Bion International Conferences who believed in me and helped develop the historical moment in 2022 in which Mexico City hosted the Bion International Conference for the first time. Thanks to Giorgio Corrente (Bion Rome, 2007), Howard B. Levine and Larry Brown (Bion Boston, 2009), Afsaneh Alisobhani and Glenda Cortorphine (Bion Los Angeles, 2014), Alessandro Bruni (Bion Milán, 2016), Mercia Fagundes (Bion Riverao Preto Brazil, 2018) and Antonia Grimalt (Bion Barcelona, 2020).

Thanks to the twelve contributors for their thoughtful and creative participation. An In Memoriam presentation took place during the International Conference in memory of outstanding and beloved colleagues who are physically not with us anymore but remained an alive presence; I owe an equal debt of appreciation to Donna Savory and Lesley Caldwell for sharing their thoughts of Chris Mawson (1953–2020), to Jeff Eaton for presenting a version of Neville Symington (1937–2019), and to Shirley Gooch and Thomas Helscher for giving a sensitive picture of James Gooch (1934–2020). At the time of the Bion International Online Conference Mexico 2022, we had the honor of listening to Antonio Sapienza, a beloved analyst from Sao Paulo. Sadly, some months ago, he passed away. However, fortunately we had the honor, as well, to listen to Carmen Mion, who presented an acknowledgment of his work. We closed with a special tribute to the two Mexican pioneers in Bion's work: José Luis González Chagoyan – my son's godfather – and Antonio Mendizábal. Both were celebrated and honored at the Bion International Conference Mexico 2022 for their innovative vision and tireless dedication to the study of Wilfred Bion's work. Their unwavering commitment to spreading Bion's work throughout my country continues to inspire generations. My gratitude also goes to Judy K. Eekhoff, and Nino Ferro.

Special thanks go to Michael Eigen for his participation and friendship.

Introduction

Jani Santamaría Linares

Dreams and dreaming are as much a part of human beings as breathing; they have aroused interest since time immemorial. From different points of view, explanations have been offered for this fascinating psychic product. Although Jean-Bertrand Pontalis reminded us that dreams retain an essential mystery (Flanders, 2015), Sigmund Freud rescued the study of dreams from mythmakers, neurologists and purveyors of the daemonic.[1] Of course, long before Freud wrote *The Interpretation of Dreams* (Freud, 1900) people were listening to dreams and trying to understand them, so dreams have been awaiting clarification for many hundred years (Blass, 2002).[2] Paraphrasing the famous Bion (1970) phrase: "thoughts exist without a thinker",[3] we could say that dreams have existed without having a dreaming apparatus to understand them.

Psychoanalysis would not exist if Freud had not paid attention to both his patient's dreams and his own; his remarkable capacity for self-analysis, as well as his illumination of the working of the unconscious as it produces its nightly creations, led him to affirm that the theory of dreams:

> occupies a special place in the history of psychoanalysis and marks a turning point; it was with it that analysis took the step from being a psychotherapeutic procedure to being a depth psychology.
>
> (Freud, 1933, p. 7)

He asserted it was on July 24, 1895, that "the secret of the dream revealed itself to Dr. Sigmund Freud" (Freud, 1985, p. 365).

This year (1895), Freud ushered in a new paradigm of creative engagement with the world, and the world never looked quite the same again. According to Grotstein (2000), Freud's discovery of the meaning of dreams "disturbed the universe".[4] He believed that *The Interpretation of Dreams* was a landmark in psychoanalysis's evolution and that it occupies a fundamental position in its episteme (p. 733). The study of *The Interpretation of Dreams* (Freud, 1900, Chapter VII, p. 509) also gave rise to the first model (topic) of the psychic apparatus with characteristics of universality (Santamaría, 2022).

In this Introduction, I will first briefly present Freud's ideas on dreams and dreamwork, before mentioning selected developments in later thinking about dreams, specifically Wilfred Bion's contributions, and then end by discussing each of the book's chapters. His conception of dreams and dreaming, in which he elaborated on, modified and extended the ideas of dreams developed by Freud, introduced a vast revolution, especially when he moved psychoanalytic theory from Freud's theory of dreamwork to a concept of dreaming in which it is the central aspect of all emotional functioning (Ogden, 2022; Schneider, 2023). As Ogden (2004, p. 577) pointed out, Bion makes a shift by moving the emphasis on dreams "from the symbolic meaning of dreams to the process of dreaming in all its forms". This paradigm shift has changed analytic work in many ways. One of these changes is our understanding of the oneiric dimensions of the mind.

Oneiric Dimensions of the Mind is the title of the Bion International Conference that took place Online in 2022. With the death of Wilfred Ruprecht Bion in Oxford on November 8, 1979, psychoanalysis lost one of its most distinguished practitioners and original thinkers; we are in debt to Parthenope Bion, his daughter, who, in July 1997, organized the first International Bion Conference in Torino, Italy (1997), to celebrate the centennial of her father's birth (September 8, 1997). This experience started a tradition that became an international forum to keep Bion's ideas alive and to build on and elaborate his thoughts (Levine and Santamaría, 2024). Also, the meetings had their features and focus but shared concerns, doubts, and the mutual experience of working with Bion's ideas (Levine, 2015). In the spirit of this tradition, A-Santamaría Psychoanalysis Mexico Association AC, (2023) a non-profit, independent psychoanalytic educational association, began organizing the first Mexican International Bion Conference to be held in person in 2022.

However, in 2020, the COVID-19 pandemic marked a paradigm shift in the history of this century and, quite possibly, in the history of this millennium. The coronavirus was not announced at the threshold of life; it entered violently, stripping the extreme fragility of the human species and opening the doors wide to the unknown (Santamaría, 2020). Bion always underlined the importance and courage of being able to lodge new ideas or unknown aspects of the personality/society in the Mind, and he also talked about the importance of *Learning from Experience* (Bion, 1984a). He also preserved in the following sentence one of the most valuable we considered necessary during the experience of COVID-19: "We must try to do, with the little we have, the best we can" (Bion, 1994, p. 245). Hence, in the face of COVID-19 and travel uncertainties, the A-Santamaría Psychoanalysis Mexico AC, as sponsor of the conference, decided to hold it online.

Gabriel García Márquez seems to have anticipated this terrible pandemic when in *One Hundred Years of Solitude* (Márquez, 2003 [1967], p. 4), he wrote: "Science has eliminated distances [...] in a short time, man will be able to see what is happening anywhere on earth without leaving his own house".

Going back to the International Conference, in 1978, a Mexican analyst traveled to Los Angeles to invite Wilfred Bion to Mexico, to which Bion replied, "I don't know exactly what activities are planned for next year, but I have been invited to India, Canada and now Mexico. It would be good to exchange letters; I'd like that" (Dupont, 1978). Forty-four years later, it was an honor to host the Bion International Conference for the first time, which symbolically gave Wilfred Bion's legacy the key to our country and filled us with great pride and joy. For four days, we were inspired by a unique virtual setting: Mexico City, home to great poets, painters, musicians and dancers, with its rich cultural heritage. Colleagues from over 29 countries were embraced online by the infinite rich spirit of our Mexican culture; we shared receptive states of reverie in a mixture of scintillating fraternal experience that produced caesuras, turbulences, fertilization and geographical expansions, and we discussed expressions of the oneiric dimensions of the mind in many aspects: in arts, in groups, in clinical work, etc.

This book brings together 12 essential and enduring contributions from colleagues of different regions to the International Conference Mexico 2022. Inspired by Bion but adding a new dimension to the understanding of dreams, dreamwork, and the oneiric dimensions of the mind, the authors shared a wide variety of contemporary clinical and theoretical explorations and extensions.

A detailed history of Freud's writings about dreams is beyond the scope of this Introduction;[5] the same goes for Bion's writings about dreamwork.[6] My intent is not to be historically complete. Rather, the aim is to address some sources of current elaborations about dreams and dreaming. What follows is a brief review of the classical theory of dreams.

Freud

The psychoanalytic theory of dreams and dreaming is as old as psychoanalysis. Freud's first major work, *The Interpretation of Dreams* (1900), laid the foundation for psychoanalytic metapsychology and has been the fundamental text and source for our understanding of the fascinating and enigmatic world of dreams for more than a century. These significant ideas were developed in 1896 during Freud's self-analysis near his father's death. Four years later, he published his most comprehensive statement on these revelations. In this book, the subtle genius presented in detail what would become the foundation and the heart of the psychoanalytic theory regarding the meaning of dreams. Lansky (1992) considers *The Interpretation of Dreams* to still holds it to be the essential introductory text in psychoanalytic training and a fundamental introduction to the psychoanalytic conception of the Mind (p. 3).

In chapter seven of *The Interpretation of Dreams*, Sigmund Freud argues that the dream is an essential and complete psychic act. The psychic apparatus he postulates is a system with a direction, sensory pole and a motor pole (according to the reflex arc model). The stimulus for forming dreams is produced predominantly in the unconscious system. However, the stimulus is also linked to latent ideas of the preconscious. In the dream, the excitation takes a topographic regressive path. Instead of propagating towards the motor pole, it does so towards the sensory pole and reaches the system of perceptions. Moreover, it has a regressive character instead of a progressive direction. Thus, dreaming is a regression to the early stages of infancy, to an original (infantile) primitive mode of mentation, called the primary process, whereby we can "hallucinate" wish fulfillments. Flanders (2015 [1993]) considered that Freud also proposed in this chapter a theory of mental organization and functioning, which seemed to explain the diverse phenomena of dream psychology, neurotic symptom formation of parapraxes, and jokes satisfactorily (p. 50).

From Freud's perspective, during sleep, there is a disconnection from the logic (and musculature) of waking life; the focus of one's attention is turned entirely to managing one's internal life (Freud, 1900, p. 608).

He goes on to say, "Aristotle was entirely right, long ago, in his modest pronouncement that dreams are the mental activity of the sleeper" (Freud, 1917, p. 234).

Freud considered dreams to serve the psychological function of keeping the sleeper from being overwhelmed by disturbing thoughts. He states: "There is only one useful task, only one function, that can be ascribed to a dream, and that is the guardian of sleep from interruption" (Freud, 1925, p. 127). He believed that dreaming's ultimate purpose is to guarantee sleep by "converting conflicts into wish-fulfillments and thereby keeping the latent dream thoughts unconscious to protect System Cs from them" (Freud, 1900, p. 615).

Although Freud initially presented a complex model of dreaming, the emphasis of this model was on the wish. In chapter five of *The Interpretation of Dreams*, Freud emphasized the unconscious as a dreamer instigator that is only stimulated by the day's residue. He wrote in 1900, "The entrepreneur of a daytime thought requires the capital of a wish from the unconscious" (Freud, 1900, p. 561).

The component operations of dreaming are identical to those Freud (1911) associates with the primary processes. Freud perceived dreams as generated by sexual and aggressive impulses or their psychological representatives and considered that every dream owes its content to both past (infantile wishes and drives, seeking gratification) and present. In order to find an avenue for discharge and yet still preserve sleep (since direct discharge would awaken the dreamer), these wishes attach themselves to a day's event, referred to as the day's residue, and are then disguised through what he called dreamwork; "dreamwork removes (disarticulates) the conjunctive links between thoughts and then reverses the hierarchy of their importance by placing the more emotionally experienced ideas in the background and the less important ones in the foreground" (Freud 1900, p. 445).

To dreamwork (in chapter six), Freud (1900) assigned the following three operations:

- Condensation: "the dream collapses several concepts into one for purposes of disguise" (Freud, 1900, p. 171). As a result of condensation, one element in the manifest dream may correspond to numerous elements in the latent dream thoughts, but conversely, one element in the dream thoughts may be represented by several images in the dream.
- Displacement: "replacing something by an allusion which is more remote" (Freud, 1900, p. 174). Displacement shifts the accents; ideas are separated from the effects attached to them, and the effects are dealt with independently.
- Representation: "transforming thoughts into visual images" (Freud, 1900, p. 175). The creation of visual means of representations of the logical relations between the dismembered dream thoughts by the dream work, and considerations of representability – including the use of symbols and sensory, mainly visual, images (1900, p. 445).

A further variable comes into play: we add a secondary revision to this almost complete process (1900, p. 449). The secondary process refers to the later and more highly developed conceptual, logical and structured mode of mentation and uses symbols. In terms of dreamwork, a compromise is achieved between the repressing forces and the repressed, and a forbidden wish can find fulfillment without disturbing the repressing agencies. Censorship forbids unconscious impulse expression in forms they would naturally assume.

In summary, a dream is formed only when current events (day residues) contact an impulse from the past – specifically, an infantile wish. The driving force is always realizing a desire, and its function is preserving the dream.

This topic leads us to another important contribution: when we refer to dreams theoretically, we have three distinct entities in Mind: the manifest dream, latent dream, and dreamwork. Freud states: "The manifest content of the dream is the result of dreamwork, and the analytic task is to retranslate it as to be able to learn its latent content" (Freud, 1900, pp. 652–661).

For Blass (2002), Sigmund Freud discovered the meaning of the meaningless and revealed the Mind's secrets that seem to elude comprehension. In her opinion, Freud's great discovery was that meaningful statements contained in the dream could be revealed by applying the psychoanalytic method (Blass, 2002, p. 201).[7] In other words, it was not until Freud's work that the interpretation of dreams became a therapeutic technique. At the end of Part E in the seventh chapter of *The Interpretation of Dreams*, Freud throws into relief the famous phrase: "Dreams are the royal road to a knowledge of the unconscious activities of the mind" (Freud, 1900, p. 608). This phrase took him to his landmark contribution of the method of dream interpretation.

The method Freud developed for interpreting dreams draws from the technique he and his mentor Josef Breuer evolved from treating psychopathology, through which unraveling symptoms back to their origins coincided with the symptom's extinction (Sugarman, 2023, p. 23).

Chapters two to six of *The Interpretation of Dreams* outline the clinical material addressing the associative method. It is in the clinical centerpiece "Specimen Dream: Irma's Paradigmatic Dream" (chapter two) that Freud proposed the well-known "molecular method", which consists of deciphering the dream, sentence by sentence, with the help of the narrative created by the patient's associations. He consistently sustained that the dream's meaning is not in the manifest or surface content of the remembered dream and instead insisted on the importance of opening up the network of the dreamer's associations to fragments of the dream.

In considering the idea of the manifest dream, Jimenez (2012) discusses how contemporary clinicians have an understanding of the manifest dream that is different from the classic interpretations; the author reminds us that dreams are not built on "static interpretations of dream symbols" or exclusively on the patient's associations. In dual psychoanalytic practice, most clinicians use an interplay of manifest and latent content.

Freud's work continued a focus on dreaming with the paper "A Metapsychological Supplement to the Theory of Dreams" (Freud, 1917), in which, in agreement with Aristotle, he asserted that dreaming was a kind of thinking, the product of the way that the mind worked during sleep. Twenty years after the publication of *The Interpretation of Dreams*, in *Beyond the Pleasure Principle* (Freud, 1920), he addressed: "… It is, therefore, impossible to clarify as wish fulfilments the dreams which occur in either the 'traumatic neurosis' or the dreams during psychoanalysis which bring to memory the physical trauma of childhood" (Freud, 1920, p. 32).[8]

Freud never fully re-wrote the theory of dream interpretation to bring it entirely within the framework of later conceptualizations; however, in 1938, the ground of dream interpretation shifted: the dream was seen to reproduce conflict between dynamic agencies in the Mind and with the subsequent development of the tripartite structural theory (Freud, 1923). With the subsequent development of the tripartite structural theory (Arlow and Brenner, 1964), dreaming is viewed more as an expression of intrapsychic conflicts between three psychic agencies.

Related to the manifest dream, a number of theoretical and clinical contributions demonstrated that the manifest content is itself revelatory of meaning (Erikson, 1954; Kohut, 1971).[9] Ego psychology emphasis on synthesis and adaptation, for instance, and the adaptive function of the ego, specifically as it is manifest in the dream, is the subject matter of these contributions. On the other hand, the emphasis on self-state dreams is later developed by Kohut (1977) and his followers, marking a significant separate development in psychoanalysis.

Therefore, the manifest dream should not only be considered an envelope for its latent content. The content of the latent dream may also contain important unconscious meanings concerning early object relationships, conflicts, anxieties, etc. Much earlier, Jung (1954) had suggested that "The manifest dream picture is the dream itself and contains the whole meaning of the dream" (p. 149).

Later contributions developed Freud's insight even further, and dream theories assumed a new form from the 1930s onwards, owing to changes in the theory of Mind. *The Interpretation of Dreams* thus occupies a prominent place in the history of models of the Mind (Kafka, 2002).

Mancia (1988) argues that Klein must take credit for intuitively grasping the profound analogies between the language of play and that of dreams, both being archaic and able to express themselves in images. Consequently, dreams took on a central function – namely, that of representing the various phases towards which the Mind tends during its development; for with the theory of internal objects, the human Mind can be represented as a private theatre (Mancia, 1988) in which characters interrelate, and conflicts and defenses generate meaning that is projected on to the outside world and interpersonal relations (p. 1209). In this sense, Segal (1992) continued Klein's idea of playing-dreaming, the attention of the world of dreams opened up by Freud, and was increasingly drawn to the form and function of dreaming rather than the dream content (Segal, 1992). This view is relevant to the Kleinian analytic technique, which links dreams to the transference-countertransference in the here and now of the session. Meltzer (1984), for instance, in his book on oneiric life, affirmed that even without associative elaboration, the manifest content of the dream could offer analysts a window into the psychic reality of the patient.

Lastly, from a different perspective, the contributions found by neuroscientists to be implicated in dreaming extend the purposes of the paper; however, it is a subject that deserves further study.[10]

Concluding Reflections

A further implication of this study for dream analysis is that the dream is a special context not only in terms of the discovery of meaning but also of experience (Blass, 2002).

Different psychoanalytic models of dream interpretation have emerged in an attempt to understand dreams; dreams are valid for all psychological processes and are multiply determined and have multiple functions and meanings. There are many modes in which dreams may be described or listened to. Thus, the dream theory is, in effect, an application of general psychoanalytic thought and method to the dream rather than an independent theory with its own methods (Blass, 2002).

In conclusion, we still need to exhaust the possibility of understanding Freud's world of dreams. His masterly contributions transport us on a fascinating voyage into understanding dreams and the human Mind. Having presented a quick view of Freud's masterpiece, let's focus on some of Wilfred Bion's main ideas about dreaming.

Bion

More than a hundred years after Freud's great work, *The Interpretation of Dreams* (1900), we recognize that various new dimensions have been added to his thoughts – the next notable step after Freud's fundamental discoveries was made in the late '50s by Bion. Wilfred Bion, one of "the most gifted of our time" (O'Shaughnessy, 2005, p. 1523), had different readings of his work, which is a tribute to his originality and richness. The following phrase of Ferro's allows me to concentrate without further hesitation on the ideas I want to share regarding dreaming and the oneiric dimensions of the mind. Ferro states: "In the whole of Bion's work, the 'waking dream thought' (1962, p. 8) is the concept that for me is the most important and with the most significant implications" (Ferro, 2005, p. 1537).

Bion's extension of Freud's theory of dreaming quietly germinated in his earlier work (Bion 1970, 1984a [1962], 1984b [1963], 1984c [1965], 1984d [1967]); his major work on dreaming was written in the private notebook, *Cogitations* (Bion, 1992 [1959]), and his contributions emerged from his observations with psychotic patients. He also relied on his *reveries* [11] and his emotional response to what his patients communicated. From this background, he formulated the concept of alpha-function (Bion, 1984a, p. 3) and implicated it as the instrument (Monteiro, 2023)[12] that works on processing emotional experiences during sleep and waking life by producing alpha elements which can be used for generating images for dream thoughts.

Bion's conception of the work of dreaming is the opposite of Freud's (1900) "dreamwork":

"Freud [1933] says Aristotle states that a dream is the way the Mind works in sleep: I say it is the way it works when awake" (Bion, 1992, p. 43).

Moreover, this is where Bion took Freud more than a step forward; Bion's (1970, 1984a) thinking was the assumption that the mental activity that produces nighttime dreams also takes place while we are awake. Dreaming, for Freud, is an occasional and local nighttime event, while for Bion dreaming is a full-time ongoing psychic activity. The dream work produces unconscious "waking dream thoughts" from the building blocks of symbolic mental life that Bion called "alpha elements". Thus, Bion (1992) differs from Freud on the origin of the dream by stating that it is an emotional experience, not the day's residue, that produces it.

In *Learning from Experience*, he stated: "Freud assumed that the interpretation, the latent content, was the origin of the dream. The origin is in an emotional experience" (Bion, 1984a, p. 135).

Bion also considered that sense impressions (imprints) of emotional Experience constitute the "first cause" in initiating dreaming; thus, dreaming accomplishes affect management. The term he gave to raw, unprocessed data is "beta elements" (Bion, 1984a, p. 26); these are sensorial sensations registered somatically but not psychically represented in any way that we ordinarily think of as "psychological".

Note that as Ferro (2006) has described, Bion:

> …turns Freud's position on dreams upside down: whereas Freud used the term 'dreamwork' to mean that otherwise incomprehensible unconscious material was transformed into dreams and that the dreamwork had to be undone to make the incomprehensible dream comprehensible again (Freud, 1933). Bion considers that conscious material must be subjected to dreamwork to render it suitable for storing away and thought.

Quoting Ogden (2004):

> Freud's dreamwork allows derivatives of the unconscious to become conscious, while Bion's work of dreaming allows conscious lived experience to become unconscious (i.e., available for the unconscious for the psychological work of generating dream-thoughts and for the dreaming of those thoughts).
>
> (p. 1356)

About dreaming,[13] Bion alludes to his belief that the sense impressions of emotional Experience that System Cs intercept must first be routed directly through the selectively permeable contact barrier into System Ucs for waking dreaming to produce making dream thoughts and then be selectively returned to System Cs for rationale thought. It is clear how Bion united the actions of the pleasure and reality principles and of the conscious and unconscious working harmoniously and complementarily. In summary, emotional Experience is the first cause of the dreaming process, not wish fulfillment; Bion describes the function of the dream as a mental digestive process in which emotional truth is the dream's latent content.

Lastly, Bion (1984b) underlined the importance of visual images and the narratives (p. 74) that employ them as the product of alpha-function. Grotstein (2009) explained it this way: "Bion's theory of dreaming seems to hint at being a hologram, i.e., a three-dimensional image in which each pixel within the image comprises the whole image, like the chromosome located in each cell of the body" (p. 746).

I cannot extend Ferro's unique contributions in "Transformations in Dreaming and Characters in the Psychoanalytic Field" (Ferro, 2009) but may say that Ferro furthered this focus, conceiving that the visual images produced by dreaming accumulate into pictograms or narratives, which become organized into the dream's narrations.

Ferro illustrates:

> ... dreaming is a constant activity carried out by our psychic apparatus, even when we are awake. This state means that the mental work of wakefulness consists of forming images that sum up, just as in night dreams, the emotional quality of what we are living at that moment. What we "say" is the narrative of these images.
>
> (2005, p. 429)

Bion's idea that the "analyst must dream the (analytic) session" registers in *Cogitations*: "these events [of the session] are having something done to them mentally, and that which is being done must be able to dream the session" (Bion, 1992, p. 120).

This idea has been picked up in the analytic world, and we now hear, for example, of the analyst's dreaming the patient's dream (Abel-Hirsch, 2016; Cassorla, 2018; Ogden, 2004). To illustrate, the idea of dreaming the analytic session, for Ogden (2022) is one of the most important and one of the most difficult psychoanalytic concepts, "when the analyst dreams the event of the session with the session, he transforms consciously perceived experience into unconscious experience" (p. 99).

He wrote:

"In the Tradition of Bion (1962a, 1987, 1992) I think of dreaming as synonymous with unconscious thinking. Unconscious thinking (dream thinking, Ogden 2010) is our richest form of thinking in which experience is viewed from multiple vertices simultaneously" (p. 99).

Unfortunately, there is not enough room to review Bion's trilogy, *A Memoir of the Future*, here; the book's three volumes are "The Dream", "The Past Presented", and "The Dawn of Oblivion". I will mention Eigen (2005, 2007, 2011, 2024), who has a brilliantly original way of communicating the heart of *A Memoir of the Future*. Few people would be better qualified than him to study this masterpiece. Through his wisdom, he always offers possibilities for human experience innovatively; the clinician and the poet come together when Eigen's "dream" about his autobiographies lies atop Bion's dream about himself; the result is compelling and stunning. For Eigen (2024), *A Memoir* is a kind of waking dreamscape, a psychic play space: "voices of dream characters collide, stimulate, inseminate, bypass each other then quiet down and the dreamer sleeps" (p. 99).[14]

Williams (2009), Jenkins (2024), Grotstein (2009) and Sandler (2009), among others, have also profoundly studied *The Memoir*.

In showing the differences and similarities between Freud's and Bion's theories of dreaming, we could conclude that, as Braga (see Chapter Eight) pointed out, the traditional view of the oneiric dimension for the development of representations (dreamwork, in Freud) has been replaced by a view of a dimension encompassing several mental spaces and processes, a cradle for photo-thoughts and emotions that explores different mediums.

Space limitations also prevent me from presenting all the contributions to Bion's work by those such as Ferro, Ogden (2001, 2003, 2004, 2010), Schneider (2023), Grotstein (2000, 2009), Sandler (2009), and Monteiro, among others. These authors describe with extraordinary accuracy the multiple perspectives from which Bion's work has been studied; they all offer their work as "intercessors", using Bion's term or as "midwives", using Socrates term (Williams, 2009).

Chapter Summaries

It is challenging to present topics from this book's lively papers written by distinguished psychoanalysts. All the papers are a beautiful illustration of dealing with and thinking about the oneiric dimensions of the mind. Therefore, I will provide the background to know the plurality of topics addressed and the original perspectives in which they are set; my focus is on leaving a non-saturated space for the readers to encourage a dialogue with the readers.

The book begins with "Freud's Dream and Bion's Dream" by Howard B. Levine. His paper is dedicated to the memory of Jim Grotstein and pays tribute to Grotstein's contribution to Bion's theory of dreams, comparing Freud's understanding of the dream and dreamwork with that of Bion. Levine mentions that dreams are complex constructs of memories, perceptions and emotions. He reminds us that for Freud, the dream was a nighttime event whose functions included expressing unconscious, unsatisfied wishes and being the guardian of sleep. For Bion, dreamwork takes place continuously, whether awake or asleep, and its function is to make sense of raw existential Experience, create meaning out of "facts", and regulate psychic tension through representation and linkage. He concludes with his characteristic clarity by summarizing four points Jim Grotstein (2009) made in his seminal paper "Dreaming as A Curtain of Illusion: Revisiting the 'Royal Road' with Bion as Our Guide".

In "Bion and my Patients", the second chapter, Anne Alvarez begins by offering a vivid memory of a group seminar with Bion in London a few years before he died: "Bion began by reading us a new paper on dreams, in which he suggested that dreams should not always be seen as simply defensive or wish-fulfilling, but that real change and development could occur in the course of a dream". The author shares her Experience about a dream of a patient whom she considers got it wrong. Bion's answer helped the author learn from this unique Experience the importance of thinking much more about the difference between a defense and the realization of a dream come true. Alvarez's paper illustrates the central concept of all emotional functioning that Schneider (2023) points to as follows: "that we are alive in our dreaming and that it is dreaming that brings us to life. As Ogden (2007) pointed out, patients get their dreams analyzed with the hope of receiving help in completing the unconscious work by "talking as dreaming".

The inspiring strength of so many of Anne Alvarez's new ideas and views on dreams and dreaming makes the second chapter a new step in the insurmountably complex yet fascinating discussion of thinking about, understanding and knowing the human Mind.

In Chapter Three, "On Going Further to What We Know", Nicola Abel-Hirsch continues similarly the theme begun by Alvarez by noting that dreams also serve the function of organizing Experience. She states that in contemporary psychoanalysis, we are familiar with attending to our relation to what is not known and considers that our emphasis on the defensive nature of "knowing" however can obscure other more healthy and demanding relations to what we know. In her paper, she looks at a number of Bion's austere, assertive statements of what he knows and at the relation of these statements to his more explorative work. A clinical example of the analytic couple is given: they both go further into what they respectively knew already. Through this example, taking the focus off the relationship between patient and analyst, we observe a shift from "what the analyst knows" to what both can bear to contain.

The paper lectures us all on how susceptible, exacting and often even frightening it is to sit behind a coach. Abel-Hirsch subscribes to Bion's contribution to a new, refreshing perspective; her approach is always innovative and far-reaching.

Chapter Four, "Dreaming, Daydreaming and Sensing Things Together", is written by Peter Goldberg. He argues that the oneiric dimension is considered from the vantage point of daydreaming, which recapitulates the function of dreaming and does something different. The conditions that facilitate the shift into daydreaming are compared with how the analyst and the analytic frame function to induce an analytic state of Mind in patients and analysts. This inductive activity of the analyst works in the background of the analyst's interpretive and reverie functions. For Goldberg, the idea of day-dream-work is conceived to highlight the importance of shifts in consciousness in everyday life and in analysis, especially in providing access to collective dimensions of psychical life beyond the limitations of the individual ego. This invokes Bion's conception of O, or at-one-ment, albeit a version of at-one-ment that operates in the sensory realm. In this regard, the idea of a Beta function is proposed to capture something of importance in the psychical life of sensory patterns of shared psycho-sensory Experience. This paper provides an opportunity to think about the place of dreaming in the theory and practice of psychoanalysis today. For instance, Schneider (2023) goes on to develop the idea that all dreams are psychological works in progress, containing aspects of emotional experience that are entirely or partially too disturbing to dream on one's own.

Chapter Five, "We-ness as an Expansion of Bion's Psychoanalytic Function of Intuition", by Giuseppe Civitarese, is written with the thought-provoking style for which he is well known. Over the past several years, Civitarese has published remarkable papers that have enhanced our knowledge and understanding of dreams in a highly creative and clinically valuable way. The paper explores Bion's evolution from Kleinian psychoanalysis to a more group-oriented perspective, emphasizing the role of intuition. For Bion, intuition is a psychoanalytic function of the analyst, the principal factors of which are the various expressions of dream thought and insight. Furthermore, within the frame of the post-Bionian theory of the analytic field, the author suggests adding to these factors the use of the "we" vertex (or we-ness), i.e., to regard virtually every fact of analysis as co-created. The paper stresses the importance of practicing intuition in order to make it as spontaneous as possible. From this angle, we-ness appears as a factor in the psychoanalytic function of intuition that can enhance its effectiveness.[15]

In Chapter Six, Avner Bergstein brings us a refreshing and vital vision of oneiric dimensions in the paper entitled "'To Risk Sailing Westward to Cathay and Thence Safely Home': The Oneiric States of Mind". Leaning on Bion's thinking, as well as process philosophy and the Jewish mystical tradition, the author considers the oneiric state of Mind depicted as the Mind's capacity for perpetual movement in its quest for a truthful apprehension of reality and its unending transformations. For him, the "to and fro" movement in pursuit of the unknowable is at the heart of Bion's thinking. This is the radical notion Bion introduces into psychoanalysis, whereby the analyst aims not so much at facilitating the transformation of the unconscious into the conscious nor making the unthinkable thinkable. Instead, they facilitate the personality to extricate itself from its tendency to adopt a "thus far and no further" attitude, a rigidified imprisonment in the past or the strived-for future. This chapter has a broad significance, not only in terms of the understanding of the detailed close reading of Bion's thinking but also because it provides an opportunity to re-examine what Monteiro (2023) considers the central quality of Bion's visionary model of the Mind; Monteiro focuses on the belief that all that is interesting in the human Mind pulsates with an unreadably complex dynamic beyond the unknown, the unknowable and the unthinkable.

Chapter Seven, "A Dream Is Just a Dream", written by Rudi Vermote, offers an original perspective and is a notable work. The author's hypothesis in this chapter is that the oneiric functioning of the Mind – of which dreams are a manifestation amongst several other manifestations – corresponds with who we are: it is the stuff that we are made of. We may call it as well "the mind" or Freud's "unconscious ego". In Bion's words, it is a "transformation in Knowledge". As the title would have it, a dream is just a dream. However, the oneiric function of the Mind is to interface with the world and create ourselves and the world psychically – it is a function that is self-centered and anxiety-ridden. It blocks our contact with the infinite, unrepresented field of Being we are part of. The author discusses the dynamics between these psychic worlds and the role of dreaming in them.[16] The title of his paper reminds me of Eugene Mahon's (2022) book, *Such Stuff as Dreams: A Psychoanalytic Inquiry*, where Mahon in his title pays homage to *The Tempest*, to Prospero's lines, "We are the same stuff that dreams are made of, and in a dream culminates our brief life". They suggest that the stuff of dreams is as complexly magic as the stuff evolution has used to fashion the human "little life" out of a small quantity of life that "is rounded with a sleep" (Mahon, 2022, p. 1). Vermote provides many stimulating and engaging ideas, such as the use of words that sometimes do not fit with what we want to transmit.

The following two chapters refer to the clinical implications of Bion's ideas. Bion tried in his writings and lectures to prepare the minds of analysts for encounters with their patients; this is an idea that Levine (2015) also has pointed out. For Bion, the here-and-now of the session, especially the state and functioning of the Mind of the analyst and its degree of receptivity to the projections and needs of the patient, forms the fundamental reality of the psychoanalytic situation and serves as a central locus of analytic investigation.

With these assumptions as a starting point, in Chapter Eight, João Carlos Braga illustrates them in his paper "The Oneiric Dimensions of the Mind in the Analytic Session". Based on a psychoanalytic session, João Carlos Braga examined the oneiric dimensions of the mind in different layers of abstraction. To achieve this task, the author uses Bion's work as his psychoanalytic reference, especially the theory of transformations (Bion, 1984c). Convergently with the clinical description, the author also examines Bion's imaginative speculation of the presence in us of other senses beyond the common ones that we usually recognize.

Antonio Sapienza presents another important clinical presentation. In Chapter Nine, "Learning from the Experience in the Analytic Session: Dream Work-Alfa", the author highlights the essential qualities of the analytic couple that allow us to "dream" the ongoing session in the analysis room. Some of his most cherished themes are: the primitive mind; the always active double arrow movement between the psychotic and non-psychotic part of the personality; the importance of the permeable barrier of contact in the interplay between external and internal reality; the analyst's dream-work-alfa in learning from experience; and the four necessary conditions for the analyst's mind: ethic, compassion, truth, and contact with mental pain.

Both chapters illustrate Bion's recommendation for observing the patient; Bion believed that the analyst must combine the disciplined curiosity of the scientist, the warmth of the humanist, the wisdom of the philosopher, and the sensitivity of the artist. They also offer fresh and much-needed insights into aspects of dream life that we regularly encounter in our clinical work, and by bringing these chapters together in this volume, they have rendered an excellent service to the analytic community. Monteiro's (2023) reading of Bion also highlighted the implications of clinical encounters for the analysts that Sapienza and Braga stress in these chapters; the essential qualities of the analytical equipment that allow us to "dream" the ongoing session in the analysis room. Contemporary analysts also raise essential considerations, for instance Ferro's concept of the analytic field and Ogden's view of the functioning of the analyst's reverie and the "analytic third" (Ogden, 2001); both authors underline that dreams within an ongoing analysis involve both analyst and patient working together.[17] Chapters Eight and Nine illustrate that the analyst's mental state and the qualities of his mental functioning (no memory and desire) in a constant state of transformation seem essential; the analyst's challenge is to be sensitive to this creative and mysterious dreaming function in himself and his patient.[18]

The last section presents three chapters about the oneiric dimensions of the mind and art.

Bion began his *Transformations* (Bion, 1984c [1965]) using artistic models. Artists have known for centuries that the capacity to dream and remember dreams is part of human creativity. Throughout the centuries, many poets and playwrights, such as Shakespeare, Goethe, Calderon de la Barca, or Sor Juana Inés de la Cruz (Santamaría Fernández, 1981), were fascinated by the dream and treated the phenomena of sleeping and dreaming in multiple ways in their works. It is, therefore, not surprising that countless artists of all periods and styles also tried to capture the many and varied aspects of the dream with the help of pencil, brush and color, or with the hammer and chisel.

Dreams are also a recurrent subject of painting.[19] This is one of the many valuable ideas that Robert Snell illustrated. As a dreamer in a waking state, Snell opened all the channels of his creativity and displays in Chapter Ten an essay entitled "Cezanne Dreams Bion". In it, the author notes parallels between two pioneers in their respective fields, Cézanne and Bion. A consideration of the painter's way of working offers valuable insights into a "Bionian" approach to analytic practice. Drawing in his reserves of "Negative Capability", carried along by the flow of "Waking Dream Thought", registering the effects of even the slightest change of viewpoint, the mature Cézanne proceeded touch by colored touch, to allow the "Selected Fact" and potential "Transformation in O" to take shape. It is rare in our field for an author to explore a topic that is interesting and important for analysts, but doing so in a way that adds to our knowledge is invaluable. Moreover, it is an impressive account of Snell's thinking, grounded in many years of developments.

Chapter Eleven is entitled "Oneiric Dimensions of the Mind in Frida Kahlo". In it I offer some imaginary conjectures from which we can trace some of the oneiric dimensions of the mind in Kahlo's art. The chapter addresses Kahlo's work as a reticular experience whose meaning can slip through seven oneiric dimensions of the mind or be held in tension between various links. For this purpose, I propose the following oneiric dimensions in Frida Kahlo: familiar, pain, erogenous, social, aesthetic, finite and infinite. I parallel Bion's contributions with his masterpiece, *A Memoir of the Future* and offers Ogden's rich relation of dreaming and the container-contained as another window from which we can enter to capture the oneiric dimensions in Frida Kahlo. For Ogden, the container-contained is centrally concerned with the processing (dreaming) of thoughts derived from lived emotional experience. After sowing some seeds of thoughts and reflection for further dreams, I close by repeating Kahlo's statement: *Viva la Vida*, Long Live Life!

The last chapter, entitled "'Beatriz' and *The Great Mystical Circus*: The Musical and Poetical Transformation of an Emotional Experience", is presented by Raul Hartke and Edu Martins. In this chapter, the authors offer psychoanalytic comments about the song "Beatriz", which is the centerpiece of the musical *O Grande Circo Místico* ("The Great Mystical Circus"), with music by Edu Lobo and lyrics by Chico Buarque de Holanda. The composer and lyricist of "Beatriz" fruitfully integrate words and music, transforming them into sensory representations of the ineffable emotional Experience of the main character in the show. From the perspective of Donald Meltzer's theory of the aesthetic object, they delve into the musical and poetical techniques employed by the authors to express that emotional Experience.

Final Reflections

This book demonstrates the multifaceted fertility of Wilfred Bion's ideas about the oneiric dimensions of the mind. Thanks to these twelve contributors, we can see how his legacy flourishes in many fields. I hope that the reader finds in these pages many stimulating contributions that are fascinating studies and also demonstrate the enduring creative genius of Bion.

The authors, dreamers in "waking states", have opened all the channels of their creativity and broadened their knowledge of the importance of Wilfred R. Bion's dream work and oneiric dimensions of the mind. Providing renewed insight into psychoanalytical understandings of dreams, this book is essential reading for any psychoanalyst wishing to study dreaming as a factor of growth and evolution.

To consider the oneiric as a consistently active presence in our work (and life) allows us to open the door to new experiences, find new meanings and understand/discover something unexpected; to feel and tolerate the emotional storm of being mentally in touch with someone else. Therefore, dreaming should live in the core of the Experience of hope.

To conclude, there is an expression from Grotstein (2007) that I found extraordinarily suggestive to follow while reading this book; Grotstein picked it up from his analysis with Bion, who had said: "Do not try to understand me! Pay attention to your emotional responses to me!" (p. 8).

Therefore: do not try to understand the chapters of this book, pay attention to your dreams while reading it and get out your colors. Oneiric gates are always opened, and the musical dimensions of the Mind move vigorously. Let us allow the wind of dreams – as promoters of life – to transport the seeds of Bion to each fertile plot of land so that they permeate all generations.

Notes

1. Chapter One of *The Interpretation of the Dreams*, written just before its publication in 1900, is a lengthy consideration of other authors' writings.
2. Atemidoro's book is important in its own right; he collected dreams all over Greece, Asia Minor and Italy around AD 200. See: Artemidorus (2020) *The Interpretation of Dreams* (2020), edited by Peter Thonemann.
3. In *Attention and Interpretation* (1970), Bion nominates the pre-conception of Thought without a Thinker.
4. Freud declared that his theory of dreams "disturbed the sleep of the world" (Freud, 1900, p. 21).
5. A list of these writings is in Appendix B to *The Interpretation of the Dreams* in the Standard Edition.
6. See Ogden, 2003, for a clinical and theoretical discussion of Bion's conception of dreaming.
7. Blass (2002) offers scientific and philosophical support to Freudian claims that dreams are meaningful and that their meanings can be discovered through dream interpretation.
8. This shift in Freud's fertile thinking provided an epistemological leap for his theory of Mind, though not particularly for the theory of dreams.
9. The rich bibliography on dream analysis from Freud onwards, including the now classic works of Sharpe (1961), Erikson (1954), Anzieu (1986), and Grinstein (1983), among others, provides invaluable sources on the technique of interpretation.
10. For the relation of the dream between neuroscience and psychoanalysis, see Mancia (1999).
11. *Reverie* for Bion (1984a) is the waking dream to which the analyst makes himself available as a way in which to intuit the unconscious aspect of what is occurring at any given moment in the analytic session.
12. Monteiro (2023) postulates Bion's thinking, as a unified theory of dreams which extends and has further implications as a visionary model of the Mind.
13. "Much has been written on what dreams mean; relatively little on what it means to dream; and still less on what it means not to be able to dream" (Ogden, 2003, p. 17).
14. I am grateful to Keri Cohen (Cohen and Fuchsman, 2021), who generously shared Eigen's references about *A Memoir of the Future*. Eigen has run a study group about *A Memoir of the Future* for over 50 years.
15. "The singular being is always a plural being" (Civitarese and Ferro, quoted by Snell, 2023, p. 50).
16. Grotstein wrote: "The dreamer who dreams the dream is the ineffable subject of being" (2000, p. 46).
17. In his book *This Art of Psychoanalysis*, Ogden (2005) offers a unique contribution of psychoanalysis that features a new way of conceptualizing the role of dreams, where patient and analyst think, talk and dream previously undreamt or interrupted dreams.
18. The patient is considered to be "the best colleague" (Bion, 1978).

19 Brown (2019) wrote a short biographical study of the British landscape painter J. M.W. Turner with relation to Bion and the sublime.
20 In this book, the abbreviation *SE* is used for *The Standard Edition of the Complete Psychological Works of Sigmund Freud*, (ed.) J. Strachey. London: Hogarth, 1981.

References

Abel-Hirsch, N. (2016). Bion, Alpha Function and the Unconscious Mind. *British Journal of Psychotherapy*, 32(2), 215–225.
Alisobhani, A & Corstorphine, G. (2019). *Explorations in Bion's "O": Everything We Know Nothing About*. Routledge.
Anzieu, D. (1986). *Freud's Self Analysis*. Hogarth.
Arlow, J.A. and Brenner, C. (1964). *Psychoanalytic Concepts and the Structural Theory*. International Universities Press.
Artemidorus. (2020). *The Interpretation of Dreams*. Translated by M. Hammond, ed. P. Thonemann. Oxford University Press.
Bion, W.R. (1970). *Attention and Interpretation*. Tavistock.
Bion, W.R. (1978). *Four Discussions with W.R. Bion*. Clunie Press.
Bion, W.R. (1981). *A Key to a Memoir of the Future*. Clunie Press.
Bion, W.R. (1984a). *Learning from Experience*. Tavistock. (Original work published 1962)
Bion, W.R. (1984b). *Elements of Psychoanalysis*. Karnac. (Original work published 1963)
Bion, W.R. (1984c). *Transformations*. Karnac. (Original work published 1965)
Bion, W.R. (1984d). *Second Thoughts*. Karnac. (Original work published 1967)
Bion, W.R. (1987). *Clinical Seminars and Four Papers*. Fleetwood Press.
Bion, W.R. (1991). *A Memoir of the Future* (vol. I: The Dream). Karnac. (Original work published 1975)
Bion, W.R. (1992). *Cogitations*. Karnac. (Original work published 1959)
Bion, W.R. (1994). Making the Best of a Bad Job. In *Clinical Seminars and Other Works*. Karnac. (Original work published 1979)
Blass, B.R. (2002). *The Meaning of the Dream in Psychoanalysis*. State University of New York Press.
Brenner, C. (1969). The dream in clinical practice. *J. Nerv. Ment. Did.*, 149, 122–132.
Breuer, J. and Freud, S. (1893). Theoretical. *Studies on Hysteria*. The Standard Edition of the Complete Psychological Works of Sigmund Freud, 2, 183–251.
Brown, L. (2019). The Unbearable Glare of Living: The Sublime, Bion's Theory of "O" and J. M. W. Turner, "Painter of Light" (n.p.). In *Transformational Process in Clinical Psychoanalysis. Dreaming, Emotions and The Present Moment*. Routledge.
Cassorla, R.M.S. (2018). *The Psychoanalyst, the Theatre of Dreams and the Clinic of Enactment*. Routledge.
Cohen, K. and Fuchsman, K. (2021). *Healing, Rebirth and the Work of Michael Eigen*. Routledge.
Dupont, M. (1978). Algunas impresiones sobre Wilfred R. Bion y texto de una entrevista. *Cuadernos de Psicoanálisis*, 2(3/4), 212–225.
Eigen, M. (2005). Dream Work. In *Emotional Storm*. Wesleyan University Press.
Eigen, M. (2011). *Contact with the Depths*. Routledge.
Eigen, M. (2024). *Bits of Psyche*. Routledge.

Erikson, E. (1954). The Dream Specimen of Psychoanalysis. *Journal of the American Psychoanal. Association* 2(1), 5–56.

Ferro, A. (1999). *Psychoanalysis as Storytelling*. Routledge.

Ferro, A. (2005). Bion: Theoretical and Clinical Observations. *International Journal of Psychoanalysis*, 86, 1535–1542.

Ferro, A. (2006). Clinical Implications of Bion's Thought. *International Journal of Psychoanalysis*, 87, 989–1003.

Ferro, A. (2009). Transformations in Dreaming and Characters in the Psychoanalytic Field. *International Journal of Psychoanalysis*, Apr, 90(2), 209–230.

Flanders, S. (2015). *The Dream Discourse Today*. The New Library of Psychoanalysis. (Original work published 1993)

Freud, S. (1985). *The Complete Letters to Wilhelm Fliess (1887–1904)*. Joseph M. Masson (ed.). Belknap Press.

Freud, S., (1900). The Interpretation of Dreams. In *The Standard Edition of the Complete Psychological Works of Sigmund Freud*, 4, ix–627. Hogarth Press.

Freud, S. (1911). Formulations on the Two Principles of Mental Functioning. SE, 12, 213–226.

Freud, S., (1917). Metapsychological Supplement to the Theory of Dreams. SE, 14, 217–235.

Freud, S., (1920). Beyond the Pleasure Principle. SE, 18, 1–64.

Freud, S., (1923). The Ego and the Id. SE, 19, 1–66.

Freud, S. (1925). Some Additional Notes on Dream-Interpretation as a Whole. SE, 19, 127–130.

Freud, S., (1933). Revision of the Theory of Dreams. In New Introductory Lectures of Psychoanalysis. SE, 22, 1–182.

García Márquez, G. (2003). *One Hundred Years of Solitude*. Harper. (Original work published 1967)

Grinstein, A. (1983). *Freud's Rules of Dream Interpretation*. International Universities Press.

Grotstein, J. (2000). *Who Is the Dreamer, Who Dreams the Dream? The Study of Psychic Presences*. Analytic Press.

Grotstein, J. (2007). What Does it Mean to Dream? Bion's Theory of Dreaming. In *A Beam of Intense Darkness: Wilfred Bion's Legacy to Psychoanalysis* (pp. 259–289). Karnac.

Grotstein, J. (2009). Dreaming as a "Curtain of Illusion": Revisiting the "Royal Road" with Bion as Our Guide. *International Journal of Psychoanalysis*, 90, 733–752.

Jenkins, T. (2024). These Old Ghosts, They Never Die: The Enduring Experience of the First World War in Bion's Late Literary and Autobiographical Writing. Paper presented at the Bion Commemoration Online Conference, July 7th.

Jimenez, J.P. (2012). The Manifest Dream is the Real Dream: The Changing Relationship between Theory and Practice in the Interpretation of Dreams. In P. Fonagy, H. Kächele, M. Leuzinger-Bohleber and D. Taylor (eds.), *The Significance of Dreams: Bridging Clinical and Extraclinical Research in Psychoanalysis* (pp. 31–48). Karnac.

Jung, C.G. (1954). The Practical Use of Dream Analysis. *Collected Works of C.G. Jung: The Practice of Psychoanalysis*, Vol. 16, pp. 139–162. Princeton University Press.

Kafka, S.J. (2002). History of Psychoanalysis: Freud and Dream Contributing to and Celebrating the Centenary of The Interpretation of Dreams as the Origin of the Psychoanalytic Method. *International Journal of Psychoanalysis*, 83, 483–486.

Kohut, H. (1971). *The Analysis of the Self.* International Universities Press.
Kohut, H. (1977). *The Restoration of the Self.* International Universities Press.
Lansky, M.R. (1992). The Legacy of the Interpretation of the Dreams. In *Essential Papers on Dreams.* New York University Press.
Levine, H. (2015). Dreaming the Patient into Being: A Methodology for Clinical Seminars. In M. Harris Williams (ed.), *Teaching Bion: Modes and Approaches.* Karnac.
Levine, H. and Brown, L. (eds.). (2013). *Looking Forward, Looking Ahead. Growth and Turbulence in the Container/Contained. Bion's Continuing Legacy.* Routledge.
Levine, H. and Santamaría, J. (eds.). (2023). *Autism Phenomena and Unrepresented States. Explorations in the Emergence of the Self.* Phoenix House.
Levine, H. and Santamaría, J. (eds.). (2024). *The Bion Seminars at the A-Santamaría Association: Clinical and Theoretical Explorations.* Routledge.
Mahon, E. (2022). *Such Stuff as Dreams: A Psychoanalytic Inquiry.* International Psychoanalytic Books.
Mancia, M. (1988). The Dream as Religion of the Mind. *International Journal of Psychoanalysis,* 69, 419–426.
Mancia, M. (1999). Psychoanalysis ant the Neurosciences: A Topical Debate on Dreams. *International Journal of Psychoanalysis,* 80, 1205–1213.
Meltzer, D. (1984). *Dream-Life: A Re-examination of the Psycho-analytical Theory and Technique.* Clunie.
Monteiro, J.S. (2023). *Bion's Theory of Dreams. A Visionary Model of the Mind.* Routledge.
Ogden, T. (2001). *Conversations on the Frontier of Dreaming.* NJ Aronson.
Ogden, T. (2003). On Not Being Able to Dream. *International Journal of Psychoanalysis,* 84, 17–30.
Ogden, T. (2004). On Holding and Containing, Being and Dreaming. *International Journal of Psychoanalysis,* 85, 1349–1364.
Ogden, T. (2005). *This Art of Psychoanalysis: Dreaming Undreamt Dreams and Interrupted Cries.* Routledge.
Ogden, T.H. (2007). On Talking-as-Dreaming. *International Journal of Psychoanalysis,* 88, 575–589.
Ogden, T. (2010). On Three Forms of Thinking: Magical Thinking, Dream Thinking and Transformative Thinking. *Psychoanalytic Quarterly,* 79, 317–347.
Ogden, T. (2022) *Coming to Life in the Consulting Room. Toward a New Analytic Sensibility.* Routledge.
O'Shaughnessy, E. (2005). Whose Bion? *International Journal of Psychoanalysis,* 86, 1523–1528.
Sandler, P.C. (2009). *A Clinical Application of Bion's Concepts: Dreaming, Transformation, Containment and Change.* Karnac.
Santamaría, J. (2020) La Experiencia del COVID 19 como continente y/o contenido. *Revista Argentina de Psicoanálisis,* 77(4), 89–97.
Santamaría, J. (2022). Horizontes Clínicos en la Obra de Bion. Contribuciones a los sueños y el soñar en la sala de análisis. In H. Katz (ed.), *Psicoanálisis en Pandemia y Post-Pandemia: Caos - Fronteras complejas - Horizontes inciertos* (pp. 115–128). Ricardo Vergara.
Santamaría Fernández, A. (1981). "El sueño. Primero sueño" de Sor Juana Inés de la Cruz. *Cuadernos de Psicoanálisis,* 14(1–4),230–248.

Santamaría Fernández, A. (1983). Los sueños contratransferenciales. El sueño de Irma. *Cuadernos de Psicoanálisis*, 16(3/4), 103–115.
Schneider, J. (2023). *Dreaming and Being Dreamt. The Psychoanalytic Functions of Dreams*. Routledge.
Schneider, J. (2010). From Freud's Dream-Work to Bion's Work of Dreaming: The Changing Conception of Dreaming in Psychoanalytic Theory. *International Journal of Psychoanalysis*, 91, 521–540.
Segal, H. (1992). The Function of Dreams. The Legacy of the Interpretation of the Dreams. In M.R. Lansky (ed.), *Essential Papers on Dreams*. New York University Press.
Sharpe, E.F. (1961). *Dream Analysis: A Practical Handbook of Psychoanalysis*. Karnac.
Sharpe, E.F. (1978). *Dream Analysis*. Hogarth. (Original work published 1937)
Snell, R. (2023). *Antonino Ferro. An Introduction*. Karnac.
Sugarman, S. (2023). *Freud's Interpretation of Dreams. A Reappraisal*. Cambridge University Press.
Thonemann, P. (2020). *An Ancient Dream Manual. Artemidorus' The Interpretation of Dreams*. Oxford University Press.
Williams, M. (2009). *Bion's Dream: A Reading of the Autobiographies*. Routledge.
Williams, M. (2015). *Teaching Bion: Modes and Approaches*. Karnac.

Chapter 1

Freud's Dream and Bion's Dream

Howard B. Levine

I

Bion "established ... a numinous science based on the abandonment of memory, desire, understanding, and a respect for relativity, complexity, and uncertainty" (Grotstein 2007, 24).

His model and sense of dreaming is central to psychic regulatory functioning – including affect containment and meaning making – and the way in which we continuously create and claim an identity and sense of self. It is this central, regulatory function that I believe Bion had in mind when he asserted that dreamwork was not just something that produces the nighttime phenomena associated with REM sleep that we call "dreams", but instead is operational 24/7 whether awake or asleep. What I hope to show is that from the perspective of Bion's descriptions of the process and function of dreaming, much of Freud's writings can be seen as a tentative movement in a similar direction.

I'd like to dedicate this chapter to the memory of Jim Grotstein and pay tribute to his explication of Bion's theory of dreams and dreaming, especially as Jim described it in his 2009 IJP paper, "Dreaming as a 'Curtain of Illusion': Revisiting the 'Royal Road' with Bion as Our Guide". In fact, this essay might well be entitled "Revisiting Bion's thinking about dreams and dreaming with *Grotstein* as our guide". As an opening epigram, I have chosen a quote from Grotstein's (2007) classic book, *A Beam of Intense Darkness: Wilfred Bion's Legacy to Psychoanalysis*, because it implies a great deal about the broad sweep of Bion's writings and the unique aim of psychoanalysis: the struggle to recognize, claim and become more of our selves.

Jim wrote:

> We spend and too often waste a lifetime walking in the shadow of our ultimate unclaimed self.
>
> (Grotstein, 2007, p. 25)

Deftly alluded to in this quote, in the word "shadow", is a reference to Plato and the epistemological assertion that we cannot ever directly and fully know the true essence of who and what we are or what we encounter in the world (the thing-in-itself, what Bion called O). What we can come to believe that we know (K) are the impressions that these things-in-themselves may be involved in producing, like the shadows on the cave wall cast by an unseen – and unseeable – fire.[1]

Bion recognized that there was an infinite dimension, O, to human experience that was unaccounted for by the then contemporary applications and understandings of Kleinian and Freudian theory. The on-going existential challenge that each of us faces and a central problematic of every analysis is how to increasingly experience and make sense of the derivatives of that infinite dimension in the process of constructing and integrating a unique personal idiom and sense of self.[2] Grotstein (2007) noted that in Bion's attempt to articulate and address this challenge, he

> moved Kleinian analysis from its basis in certainty to … uncertainty, complexity, and infinity.
>
> (p. 41)

He further suggested that there may have been an important personal stake involved in Bion's initiating this move:

> Passages in Bion's autobiography (1982, 1985) and in *Memoir of the Future* [1991] … seem … to hint at something that was missing in his analysis with Klein, and I cannot help wondering whether he spent the rest of his career trying to chart the unknown landscape of inner and outer cosmic uncertainty that he felt his analysis should have explored.
>
> (Grotstein, 2007, p. 40)

In contrast to Klein's theory, which was based on an epistemology of positivism centered on the life and death instincts,

> Bion needed … infinite dimensions to embrace, countenance, or grasp the inner cosmic uncertainty that plagued him all his life and the ghastly, traumatic "black holes" into which his fate had placed him.
>
> (Grotstein, 2007, p. 40)

Whatever Bion's motivations, in contrast to a vertex of thinking that assumes that there is an exact identity between the perceiver (subject) and the perceived (object), the thinker and the thought, Bion assumed a difference or separation. (Grotstein, 2007, p. 55).[3] As a result, Bion's

> quest for the holy grail of psychoanalytic precision changed to a stoic acceptance of uncertainty, the ultimate result being his psychoanalytic metatheory, arguably the most far-reaching paradigm shift in

> psychoanalytic history and the most suitable one to date to anticipate the newer era of relativism, probabilism and uncertainty.
>
> (Grotstein, 2007, p. 16)

This shift

> not only revolutionized psychoanalytic metapsychology and brought it back into alignment with nineteenth-century metaphysics and twentieth-century ontology (existentialism), ... [it] also perforated the proud mystique of "objectivity" that had been so sacred to logical-positivistic, deterministic science – the "scientific Establishment that had so intimidated Freud.
>
> (Grotstein, 2007, p. 23)

In so doing, Bion

> was the first to establish ... a numinous science based on the abandonment of memory, desire, understanding, and a respect for relativity, complexity, and uncertainty.
>
> (Grotstein, 2007, 24)

What I wish to emphasize is that dreaming, in Bion's model and sense of the term, is central to psychic regulatory functioning – including affect containment and meaning making – and the way in which we continuously create and claim an identity and sense of self. It is this central, regulatory function that I believe Bion had in mind when he asserted that dreamwork was not just something that produces the nighttime phenomena associated with REM sleep that we call "dreams", but instead is operational 24/7 whether awake or asleep. I also wish to show, from the perspective of Bion's descriptions of the process and function of dreaming, how much of Freud's writings can be seen as a tentative movement in a similar direction.

II

The more you look at Bion's theory of dreaming, the more it seems to be almost synonymous with a description of normative psychic functioning.

> Alpha is concerned with, and is identical with, unconscious waking thinking designed, as a part of the reality principle, to aid in the task of real, as opposed to pathological modification of frustration.
>
> (Bion, 1992, p. 54)

Considerations of "dreaming", the oneiric functioning of the mind, take us into almost every corner of Bion's thought: alpha elements, beta elements and alpha function; projective identification as communication, reverie and container/contained; the contact barrier and beta screen; O, K and the theory of transformations; and the whole of psychic regulatory functioning. Dreamwork alpha is "essential to [such functions as] attention, storage of memory, thinking, the positions [PS and D], consciousness attached to sense organs, notation, passing of judgement, motor discharge" (Bion, 1992, p. 54).

Bion's dreamwork is – or touches upon – a theory of psychic formation, evolution and functioning, a theory that can inform and guide analytic technique and that describes therapeutic action in the analytic situation. It is also a theory of *meaning making*.

> ... alpha-function is the instrument (model) that works on processing emotional experiences during sleep *and* waking life by producing alpha-elements which can be used for generating images for dream thoughts so as to render the emotional experiences *personally meaningful*. ... dreaming is an agent of our personal subjectivity.
>
> (Grotstein, 2009, p. 734)

In the Strachey translation of the Standard Edition, it is not always clear when the term dream is used, if Freud in the original German is talking about the dream *content* or the dream *process*. This distinction is much clearer in Bion, where he talks mostly about process, using such designations as dreamwork, dreamwork alpha, alpha function, transformations, etc. Consequently, in comparing Freud's and Bion's starting points in regard to the *work* of dreaming, it is useful to note that Freud's focus was divided between dream process, dream content – the origin and meaning of dreams – and what dreams might reveal about the structure of neurotic symptoms.

In contrast, Bion (1992) wrote:

> Freud assumed that the interpretation, the latent content, was the origin of the dream, and that it had been worked on by the dream-work to produce the dream. I say the origin is an emotional experience – *perhaps even an experience that is emotional and nothing else and that this is worked on* (rationalized?) to produce the dream, the manifest content as we know it, and that it is the *analyst* who then does the *interpretation* to produce the so-called latent content.
>
> (p. 135, italics added)

It is true that Freud (1900) also said a great deal about how he thought a dream (content) came into existence and that its *raison d'etre* included the preservation of the dreamer's state of sleep. However, these metapsychological deliberations seemed connected to the clinical need to detect the existence of an *already formed* unconscious desire, wish or fantasy that was hidden from awareness because of its unacceptable nature and the distress that knowing about it would produce. That is, the context of the working out of Freud's dream theory was based on his wish to show a correspondence between the unconscious representational structures that he believed existed in both dreams and neurotic symptoms and his assumption of the existence of unconscious dream thoughts, the contents of which were anxiety producing or otherwise unacceptable ideational *representations* – thoughts, wishes, fantasies and desires.

Freud (1917) reaffirmed these views in his Metapsychology of Dreams paper, when, in agreement with Aristotle,[4] he asserted that dreaming was a kind of *thinking*, the product of the way that the mind worked during sleep. This implies that dreaming is an occasional and "local" – i.e., nighttime – event; while for Bion, dreaming is a full time, on-going psychic activity.

But why does Bion say that an interpretation made by another is necessary for the creation of latent ideational psychic content? Because in Bion's model and theory, there is no fully formed, pre-existing ideational "content" in regard to either external or internal perception prior to "interpretation" (transformation).[5] The creation of this content is necessary in order to assess reality and solve problems under the aegis of the Reality Principle.

> ... without dreams you have not the means with which to think out your problem
>
> (Bion, 1954, pp. 25–26).

When the psyche of the sleeper cannot complete the act of dream formation – a normative regulatory function – then his or her sleep may be disrupted, experience cannot be noted and learned from, "sense" cannot be made of one's life. In these circumstances, self-reflection is unproductive or impossible and the production of meaningful associations and elaboration of latent and/or manifest dream thoughts may dry up. When this happens, the receptivity, reverie and alpha function of the mind of another will be required to support or supply the dreamwork needed for successful metabolization, meaning-making, self-construction and affect regulation. It is partly in regard to the analyst's coming to have intuitions and hypotheses about what might be going on and to helping the psyche of the patient resume – or develop for the first time – its capacity to do dreamwork, that Bion (1992) writes: "the analyst must dream the clinical situation" (p. 120).

Grotstein (2007), speaking of the functioning of the analyst in the analytic situation, adds the further qualification: "dreaming is an observational technique (perception itself) that is uniquely qualified to apprehend emotional qualities in oneself and the other" (p. 279).

For Bion (1962), the initial "registrations" of internal or external reality are not ideational representations in any form that can be qualified as "psychic"; they do not initially have "meaning" and cannot be thought about or put into words. They are categorized as beta elements. These can be "felt", but unless and until they are transformed by alpha-function into alpha elements, they are not yet psychic, they have no meaning and cannot be thought about or used to think with. They are in the peculiar limbo state of "turbulences" or "accretions of stimuli" that one might be aware of, but which do not yet have any meaning. In Bion's (1962, 1970) sense, they are neither conscious nor unconscious. That is, they are "sense impressions" that, prior to transformation into alpha elements, do not yet make any "sense" at all! (Levine, 2023b).

Thus, Bion revises Freud's (1900) theory of the pathway of dream-work and dream-thoughts. For Freud, the dream begins with a psychic "fact" that has force as a wish or desire. This "fact" is an organized latent dream thought that has come into psychic existence, been repressed, continues to exert pressure on the psyche through its affective and symbolic connections to other thoughts and feelings as described by Freud's description of the primary processes and achieves vicarious expression and some degree of discharge in the dream by becoming linked to and expressed by the more innocuous manifest images of the dream. For Bion, the dream begins with "an emotional experience – *perhaps even an experience that is emotional and nothing else*". This is a not-yet-processed raw, existential experience that does not by itself constitute, but may *precede*, the creation or registration of a psychic element or fact. Thus, the dream may originate in an emotional experience, presumably a beta element, or something "thalamic", something "pre-" or "proto-psychic" that is even less organized or "other" organized, more primitive, somatic without psychic registration or representation, "an experience that is emotional and nothing else."

In Bion's formulation, the analyst's mind, through contact with the patient – unconscious to unconscious; receptive via reverie to projective identification; etc. – is activated (alpha function) and creates an image (alpha element), which in turn can be used to generate a thought in the form of a narrative fragment, metaphor or personal myth through which the analyst captures his or her surmise concerning some quality of the patient's emotional state. Once this myth is constructed, felt or articulated within the mind of the analyst – i.e., once the analyst feels "certain" that this is what he or she *thinks* is happening – it may be used as data ("signals from the field") to adjust the analyst's internal listening stance and degree of activity, saturation of intervention, etc. (Ferro, 2002), or used as the basis of an interpretation that may be given directly to the patient.

So, in contrast to Freud, who at that time had the well-structured psyche of the neurotic in mind and so described an analyst who *uncovers* or *decodes* a pre-existent, hidden or otherwise formed, but disguised latent dream thought, Bion, who was more concerned with or attuned to the unstructured parts of the psyche, is describing instead how the analyst catalyzes, helps create or produces such thoughts for and with the patient through the act of interpretation. Another way of saying this is that the common understanding of Freud's description of dream formation begins with the assumption that an unacceptable representation already exists in the dynamic unconscious, while Bion assumes that only a not yet ideationally contained turbulence exists in the unstructured unconscious.

Freud's theory of the primary process in dream formation goes on to explain how displacement, condensation and symbolism work to allow for vicarious substitution for unacceptable wishes that are disguised in the form of manifest dream contents in the service of covert gratification under the aegis of the Pleasure Principle. Bion's (1992) theory of continuous dreamwork explains how transformational processes (alpha function and container/contained) work to create the basis for both conscious and unconscious representations (alpha elements that can be used to think with), the contact barrier that separates conscious from unconscious thoughts and the difference between sleep and wakefulness, and that this activity takes place in the service of the Reality Principle. Dream work "is concerned with, and is identical with, unconscious waking thinking designed, as part of the reality principle, to aid in the task of the real, as opposed to pathological, modification of frustration" (Bion, 1992, p. 54).

Grotstein (2007) linked the two, adding that dreamwork operated in the service of *both* the Pleasure and the Reality Principles in regard to that which is *both* conscious and unconscious.

III

There is much more that could and needs to be said about the recurring thread in Freud's (1950 [1895]) thinking that runs from the Project throughout his later work, especially from 1920 (*Beyond the Pleasure Principle*) onward, concerning the central role played by psychic regulatory functioning in regard to reducing and optimizing "accretions of stimuli" in the service of adaptation and the Reality Principle. This line of reasoning implicitly links Freud's intimations to Bion's later elaborations about homeostasis and container/contained.[6]

To conclude, I would like to summarize a number of points that Jim Grotstein made in his seminal 2007 paper, points that may resonate and will certainly recur and be explored throughout our conference:

1   In reconceptualizing and extending Freud's work on dreaming, Bion hypothesized that

    "we dream by day and by night and that everything we perceive consciously [sense] must be [assigned personal meaning and] taken into the unconscious via dreaming". Put another way, Bion believed that dreaming is directed as much towards one's daily experiences (day residue) [not yet processed perceptions] as towards the products of the internal world, and that the analyst must "dream" the analytic session, much as the mother must "dream" her infant's experiences. Behind this idea is Bion's belief that the *experience* of dreaming constitutes unconscious thinking.

(Grotstein, 2007, p. 39)

1   "Freud believed that dreaming was in the service of the pleasure principle.... Bion believed that dreaming was in the service of a 'joint venture' of the reality and pleasure principles to transform the raw ore of the Absolute Truth about Ultimate impersonal Reality into tolerable personal emotional reality as a mid-stage prior to thinking and objectification." (Grotstein, 2007, p. 40). Thus, dreaming, and the work of alpha function that produces what will eventuate as the dream, is "a putative transformational process that orders emotional life" (Grotstein, 2007, p. 46).

2   Freud proposed that dreams protect sleep and "subserve the pleasure principle and disguise emotional problems *while one is asleep.*" (in Grotstein, 2009, p. 735). They do this through dream-work – displacement, condensation, symbolization, representation – that transforms emotional conflicts into disguised situations of wish fulfillment. Bion proposed that dreaming is a full-time activity, 24/7, that works on sense impressions of emotional experience so as to manage affect, maintain the differentiation between sleep and wakefulness, provide a contact barrier and filter "to differentiate and protect Systems Cs. and Ucs." (Grotstein, 2009, p. 736). Dreaming "mediates the impingements of 'O', the Absolute Truth about Ultimate (and Infinite) Reality, which presents as raw sense-impressions (beta-elements) and becomes transformed by dreaming into mentalized alpha-elements. Thus it functions as a *filter* for unmentalized infinite emotional Truth" (Grotstein, 2007, p. 737). It also "resignifies past object relations and thereby promotes psychic growth by this ability to reprocess earlier experiences" (Grotstein, 2007, p. 738) [*aprés coup*]. In this sense, dreaming "is the function whereby we achieve *meaning* in context with our experiences. The *objective meaning* of events occurs atop a template of *personal emotional meaning*. The two levels of meaning cannot do without each other" (Grotstein, 2007, p. 739).

3   "... man cannot think if he cannot dream or phantasize; emotional experience is first cause for the dreaming process, not wish fulfillment, which is the defense" (Grotstein, 2007, p. 739). "... *a direct correspondence and a reciprocal relationship exist between one's capacity to dream and one's tolerance of frustration*" (Grotstein, 2007 p. 740). "... dreaming is not only a *form* of thinking; it is of the utmost importance in allowing

thinking to occur" (Grotstein, 2007, p. 741). It is "the protector, facilitator, conveyor, monitor and mediator as well as dispenser of emotional Truth in the guise of fictive imagination. It is a constant security check for our cognitive and emotional life as it quietly and mysteriously triages, prioritizes, and mediates (edits) our continuing urgencies" (Grotstein, 2007, p. 746). It *"provides us with a story for every wound and a myth for every rite of passage"* (Grotstein, 2007, p. 750).

Notes

1 For an extensive discussion of this epistemological vertex, see Levine, 2022.
2 In a Chassidic tale told by the German philosopher and theologian, Martin Buber (2002), at the moment of judgement when we are called before the throne of God to answer for how we have lived our lives, God does not ask why we were not more like Moses, or Abraham, but why were we not more like ourselves!
3 This difference between the domains of O and K is something that Bion talked about at length in *Transformations* (1965) and *Attention and Interpretation* (1970).
4 "Aristotle was entirely right, long ago, in his modest pronouncement that dreams are the mental activity of the sleeper" (Freud 1917, p. 234).
5 See Levine (2022, 2023a).
6 See for example Levine (2023a).

References

Bion, W.R. (1954). Notes on the Theory of Schizophrenic Thought. In: *Second Thoughts: Selected Papers on Psychoanalysis* (pp. 36–42). London: Heinemann.
Bion, W.R. (1962). *Learning from Experience*. London: Heinemann.
Bion, W.R. (1965). *Transformations*. London: Heinemann.
Bion, W.R. (1970). *Attention and Interpretation*. New York: Basic Books.
Bion, W.R. (1982). *The Long Week-End 1897–1919: Part of a Life*. Oxford: Fleetwood Press.
Bion, W.R. (1985). *All My Sins Remembered and The Other Side of Genius*. Abingdon: Fleetwood Press.
Bion, W.R. (1991). *A Memoir of the Future*. London: Karnac.
Bion, W.R. (1992). *Cogitations*. London: Karnac.
Buber, M. (2002). *The Way of Man*. London: Routledge Classics.
Ferro, A. (2002). *In The Analyst's Consulting Room*. London: Routledge.
Freud, S. (1900). *The Interpretation of Dreams*. S.E. 4/5. London: Hogarth Press, 1958.
Freud, S. (1917). A metapsychological supplement to the theory of dreams. *S.E.* 14: 217–235. London: Hogarth Press, 1957.
Freud, S. (1920). *Beyond the Pleasure Principle*. *S.E. 18: 3–64*. London: Hogarth Press, 1955.
Freud, S. (1950 [1895]). Project for a scientific psychology. *S.E.* 1: 281–397. London: Hogarth Press, 1966.
Grotstein, J. (2007). *A Beam of Intense Darkness. Wilfred Bion's Legacy to Psychoanalysis*. London: Karnac.

Grotstein, J. (2009). Dreaming as a 'Curtain of Illusion': Revisiting the 'Royal Road' with Bion as Our Guide. *IJPA* 90: 733–752.

Levine, H.B. (2022). *Affect, Representation and Language. Between the Silence and the Cry.* London and New York: Routledge/IPA.

Levine, H.B. (2023a). A metapsychology of the unrepresented. *Psychoanalytic Quarterly.* 92: 11–26.

Levine, H.B. (2023b). Affect, Emotion, Sensation, Feelings. Notes Towards a Metapsychology of the Psycho-Analytical Experience. In B. Ithier (ed.), *Affect and Emotion in Contemporary Psychoanalytic Practice*, pp. 31–44. London: Phoenix.

Chapter 2

Bion and My Patients

Anne Alvarez

In the late 1970s, two or three years before he returned finally to England from Los Angeles and died, Bion came to London two summers running and ran a group for Tavistock child therapists, some analysts and their spouses. The original intention had been for it to be an experiential group, but by the time we all met, Mattie Harris and Don Meltzer who had organized it – and Bion – had realized that too many of us were work colleagues for it to function as an experiential group, and so it was simply to be a discussion group. Bion began by reading us a new paper of his own dreams in which he suggested that dreams should not always be seen as simply defensive or wish-fulfilling, that in fact real change and development could take place *in the course of* a dream. I have never been able to locate this work as a published paper, and those London discussions were also never recorded or published. Bion of course had already been making it clear that, as Meltzer put it in his brilliant book, *Dreamlife*, that 'dreaming *is* thinking, that dreamlife can be viewed as a place to which we can go in our sleep when we can turn our attention fully to the internal world' (Meltzer, 1984, p. 46). Now, when we think of Klein's and Winnicott's and Segal's theory of symbolism, Bion's idea makes perfect sense in relation to some dreams, not necessarily all. If an unconscious phantasy can involve anything from a pure symbolic equation through the transitional area to something genuinely symbolic, why should not night-time phantasies called dreams be equally differentiable? (Klein, 1929; Winnicott, 1953; Segal, 1981). That is, on some occasions the thinking carried out is more successful than at others.

I will select two components or, to be precise, possible implications of Bion's paper for discussion here. The first is the conception of an ideal object as a development, not a defence, and the second is the growth of an ideal identity which can be seen, not as a projective identification, but as an anticipatory identification, therefore also as a development and not a defence.

But at first none of us had put all this together in the discussions of the paper, and I think everyone in the group was pretty startled and some disagreed with Bion. During the following week, a little boy patient of mine,

Johnny, had a dream in which he found a fossil on the patio of his house. He had clearly been thrilled. He said, 'It was wonderful, I've always wanted to touch a piece of history! But then I woke up and was so upset when I realized it was only a dream!' I knew that he and his family had been longing for a baby to be born after a miscarriage a year or so before. I went along with the idea of how sad it was that it was only a dream. But then, as the days went on, I began to remember Bion's paper, so when the group met again, I told them the story of the dream and what I now realized was probably my mistaken response. Bion indeed scolded me for it, and said, 'You could have understood that he was beginning to touch history in his analysis', that is, that he was having that experience – a real experience – in his dream. I was very moved by this, and thought about it all week. The following meeting I started to say, 'I thought differently at the time my patient told me his dream, but I have been worrying a lot as I have begun to rethink it during the week' ... I and everyone else laughed at my mistake, and as I went to go on, the person sitting next to me interrupted icily, 'Well you didn't manage it, did you?' I had not felt particularly embarrassed when I made the slip of the tongue, but now I did, and I could feel myself blushing in shame. Bion suddenly spoke and said, 'Sometimes you can make someone so afraid that they cannot think.'

Well, by then I had had a lot of analysis, but I wasn't usually easily frightened, and had never been told that before, and I think Bion's comment eventually had a quite liberating effect on my thinking.

But so did the paper. It teaches us the dangers of becoming over-reliant in psychoanalysis on the defence model of the mind. We after all owe to Klein the great meta-theoretical distinction she made between the defensive function of obsessionality, say, or manic reparation, versus the overcoming function of real reparation (I don't remember Bion mentioning the theory of symbolism, but it is clearly very relevant). Klein, and especially her follower Hanna Segal, gave us also the great theory of symbolism to which I shall return (Klein, 1929; Segal, 1981). But first let me apply and extend Bion's idea about dreams as being capable of providing an experience, i.e. learning, to the range of meanings entering into phantasies, or for that matter, into preoccupations or behaviour.

Thus we can, as I said above, place the concept of overcoming beside that of defence, but how about potency beside that of omnipotence, a sense of agency and self-respect to stand alongside narcissism; relief, joy and hope to stand alongside denial; or organization, integration, containment and regulation alongside obsessional defences against fragmentation?

To expand a bit on Segal's theory of symbolism. She pointed out that the true symbol acknowledges the otherness of the primary objects (breast, penis, mind, person), and for that matter of the symbolic representation, e.g. a violin. The self in this situation can never be, nor totally possess, the primary object, either at the Oedipal or pre-Oedipal level The process of mourning is involved, and the substitute object, e.g. the violin is also accorded its own uniqueness. In the case of the symbolic equation, on the other hand, the representation is equated with the primary object which is thus diminished in value and significance (Segal, 1981). Frances Tustin identified the nature of the 'autistic object' in terms similar to Segal's symbolic equation. Tustin pointed out that she finally realized that her little autistic patient's Austen car did not STAND FOR Tustin, it was INSTEAD OF Tustin (Tustin, 1980).

But before Bion's lesson on dreams, I was all too often seeing a patient's discovery of a new boyfriend on the weekend as A TURNING AWAY FROM the primary object in the transference, that is as a symbolic equation, when it might have been a TURNING TOWARDS a new symbolized version of that primary object. Winnicott's idea of the transitional area between the me and the not-me preceded Segal's theory but it can provide a useful midpoint, a third step between the two extremes along the dimension of levels of symbolization (Winnicott, 1953; Segal, 1957). I have subsequently added two others positions, a fourth, where the object is felt to be so remote that is neither identifiable with nor possessable, and a suggested fifth type where the apparent symbol has been perverted and its identity twisted and forced out of shape (Alvarez, 2012 pp. 154–160).

It is important to point out that Bion's (1962) own theory of alpha function has brought great enrichment to the theory of symbolism and of thinking. He suggested that thoughts precede thinking, and that alpha function is the function of the mind that makes thoughts thinkable, that lends meaning to experience. The implication is that this process of turning beta elements into alpha elements (i.e. thinkable – and linkable thoughts) occurs from birth onwards. We now know that the emotional communications made by very young babies through looks and touches are soon enriched by vocalizations and eventually by words, and gradually by thought-out words and thought-through words. One little two-year-old watching his seven-week-old baby brother make mouthing movements as the baby responded to his grandmother nodding her head and talking to him – said slowly, 'He's…trying…to…talk'. His mother agreed, and then, the next time it happened, she added slowly, 'He's listening with his mouth'. This is an interesting addition to the developmental finding that new-born babies are capable of imitation (Rizzolatti, Fogassi and Gallese, 2006). The mother was talking about something more than imitation, she was describing some sort of deep introjective, internalizing and identificatory process going on. Both mother and son were thinking as they watched and as they spoke, and in a way, so, perhaps, was the baby.

The experience seemed to be positive, yet Bion had also stressed that real learning depended on the choice between techniques for evasion and techniques for the modification of frustration (Bion, 1959). The emphasis on frustration as the motor is similar to Freud's and Kleinian ideas on separation, separateness, weaning, and absence as the great stimulators of thought (Freud, 1911; Klein, 1940; Segal, 1981; O'Shaughnessy, 1964). I wonder now whether Bion might have revised his theory in the light of his later theory of K, the desire to get to know the object (Bion, 1962). It was seen as a third motive beside love and hate. Here it is not whether the object is present, or absent, it is whether it is interesting. That baby above found his grandmother's voice and face interesting. The object was present but not fully predictable. Was it frustration or pleasure or both, but whatever it was, it definitely was not about absence or loss, or for that matter, Winnicott's illusion (1960).

But back to Bion's idea about a dream signalling growth rather than defence. I am pointing out that the issue concerns not only dreams, but phantasy. I explored the question of levels of phantasy in my first book *Live Company*, in a chapter called "The Necessary Angel, Idealization as a Development" (Alvarez, 1992). There is no mention of Bion in it. I was working on from Klein's theory of the splitting between idealized and persecutory objects. I was stressing the need for both sides of the personality to be adequately developed before integration can take place.

I started by reminding the reader of Klein's idea that integration between the bright and dark side of one's nature and of one's object is possible only when there is 'adequate development of both the idealizing and persecutory strands' (Klein, 1935). I believe there are quantitative issues here. I wrote:

> Tiny increments in the belief in an ideal object in patients whose capacity for bright hope is severely underdeveloped should not be exposed to constant reminders of the very despair and anxiety they are finally managing, not to defend against, but to overcome.
>
> (Alvarez, 1992, p. 121)

I went on to illustrate the point by describing two severely emotionally neglected boys, a very depressed 12-year-old named Ricky, and a cut-off autistic 12-year-old named Andrew. Both boys seemed, almost for the first time, to be conceiving of an ideal object, which both seemed to have seen on television. I heard about the two sessions within a week of each other, and the two therapists dealt with the material in radically different ways. Both boys had ended up by talking about a wonderful car they had seen on the television. Both started off the session very depressed and cut-off after a break from once weekly therapy. Both therapists worked very hard and sympathetically to bring them back into contact, and I believe both succeeded. The first boy suddenly perked up, changed the subject, and started telling his therapist about this amazing limousine he'd seen on the telly – It had food, tv, and even a swimming pool! It was amazing, he said, imagine having that! His therapist replied that he was imagining what it would be like to see her seven days a week instead of one, but they both knew that wasn't possible. The boy deflated and began talking about the fact that his uncle had been kicked out of his aunt's house on the weekend and was wandering around looking for somewhere to stay. He remained dejected for the rest of the session.

The second child was a very deprived boy with a damaged indented forehead from months of headbanging when left alone in his cot as a baby. After being helped out of the first 20 minutes of depression, he suddenly began describing a Rolls Royce car he'd seen on the telly. It had a window in the roof through which you could see the sky – and lots of other luxuries. His therapist took a different line from the first one, she agreed how marvellous it would be to have such a car. She thus shared the fantasy with him. He left in a much more alive and warmer mood. The first therapist saw the car as being used as a manic defence against the pain of loss, the second saw it, I think, as a moment of recovery. I would maintain that the first therapist who worked so hard to help the boy back into contact with her, didn't realize that she had succeeded, and that he was describing what it felt like now to have someone welcome him back – a someone with a capacious mind with plenty of room and resources for him. She had that model of defences against pain too uppermost in her mind, I think. The second therapist let the moment of hope and trust live and breathe and therefore persist for a while. The question arises in treating such children, is psychoanalysis only about helping the patient to understand his disturbance, or is it sometimes about re-writing a new history? Is there only conflict and denial, or is there sometimes something really missing in the mind which is finally being provided?

It is saddening that both therapists, by careful sensitive work in the first part of the session, brought their patients to the point of conceiving of a delightfully spacious, protective and available object which was felt to be specially for them, but took such different views of its meaning when it finally arrived on the scene. As I said, there is no mention of Bion's view of dreams in my chapter. I wonder if most of the time I had kept Bion's view in some idealized, slightly untouchable jewel box in my mind, while perhaps unconsciously borrowing or stealing from it.

However, in a later chapter in my book ("Wildest Dreams and Lies: Aspiration and Identification in Depressed Children", there is a discussion of the distinction between a phantasied but defensive projective identification, and a phantasied healthy anticipatory identification (Alvarez, 1992, p. 176). Here, I did draw attention to Bion's view that dreams could be something more than attempts to rewrite the past, they could involve lived experience. I cited three examples of children who seemed to be, not stealing nor faking a new desirable identity, but *trying it on in the eyes of the other.*

The first was Tommy, a boy in a state of high anxiety over a move to a distant city known for its rough reputation. At the start of the session he tried on a Marine mask he had brought. I took it up first as a defence against the fear we both knew he had. He panicked. Then, a little later, he tried it on again, and I began to comment that perhaps he was showing me that I should imagine him as strong and brave enough to cope in the new environment. He agreed, seeming very relieved.

Another patient, an adolescent girl who had been rejected both by her birth family and several foster families, tried to persuade her therapist that a photograph she'd brought was that of her uncle. The therapist began, like me, by seeing the 'uncle' as a defence against the fact that she lacked both a home and a family. Later, when the therapist could understand that she was being invited to *believe in* her patient's capacity to acquire a family, Carol could move on. But I think that someone had to hold the hope for her first. Bion had spoken of the anticipatory and prospective elements in some dreams, and so I began to think of Carol's pretending to have an uncle and Tommy's mask as anticipatory, not projective, identifications. Goethe wrote, 'Let me be attired as an angel until I become one' (Bird and Stokes, 1976).

I have discussed two possible implications deriving from Bion's theory of dreams as lived experience. These suggest that both a phantasied or dreamed conception of an ideal object and of the growth of an ideal self via an anticipatory identification, can, under certain conditions be seen as developments, not defences.

References

Alvarez, A. (1992). *Live Company, Psychoanalytic Psychotherapy with Autistic, Borderline, Deprived and Abused Children*. London and New York, Routledge.
Alvarez, A. (2012). *The Thinking Heart: Three Levels of Psychoanalytic Therapy with Disturbed children*. London: Routledge.
Bion, W. R. (1959). 'Attacks on linking'. In *Second Thoughts: Selected Papers on Psychoanalysis*. London: Heinemann.
Bion, W. R. (1962). *Learning from Experience*. London: Heinemann.
Bird, G, and Stokes, R. (1976). *The Fischer - Dieskau Book of Lieder*. London: Victor Gollancz.
Freud, S. (1911). *Formulations on the two principles of mental functioning*. In *SE*, 12, 213–226.
Klein, M. (1929). Infantile anxiety situations reflected in a work of art and the creative impulse. *International Journal of Psycho-analysis*, 21: 125–153.
Klein, M. (1935). 'A contribution to the psychogenesis of manic-depressive states'. In *The Writings of Melanie Klein*, Volume III: Envy and Gratitude and Other Works (1975). London: Hogarth.
Klein, M. (1940). 'Mourning and its relation to manic-depressive states'. In *The Writings of Melanie Klein*, Volume III: Envy and Gratitude and Other Works (1975). London: Hogarth.
Meltzer, D. (1984). *Dreamlife*. Perthshire: Clunie Press.
O'Shaughnessy, E. (1964). 'The absent object', *Journal of Child Psychotherapy*, 1(2), 34–43.

Rizzolatti G, Fogassi, L., and Gallese, V., (2006). Mirrors in the mind: Mirror neurons, a special class of cells in the brain, may mediate our ability to mimic, learn and understand the actions of others. *Scientific American*, 295 (5), 54–61.

Segal, H. (1981). *The Work of Hanna Segal*. New York: Aronson.

Tustin, F. (1980). 'Autistic objects', *International Review of Psychoanalysis*, 7: 27–39.

Winnicott, D. W. (1953) 'Transitional objects and transitional phenomena: a study of the first not-me possession', *International Journal of Psychoanalysis*, 34: 89–97.

Winnicott, D. W. (1960). 'The theory of the parent-infant relationship'. In *The Maturational Processes and the Facilitating Environment*. London: Hogarth.

Chapter 3

On Going Further to What We Know

Nicola Abel-Hirsch

Preparing my chapter for this book (some months after the conference), I could better see that it didn't wholly make sense. I was trying to work something out, but hadn't managed to be clear enough in what this was. What was I trying to work out? In contemporary psychoanalysis we are familiar with attending to our relation to what is not known. What about our relation to what we do know? In the second half of the 1960s, Bion spoke of 'knowing-about' as a defensive kind of knowing. By this he meant holding 'knowledge' as a possession that would defensively protect us against the unknown and against being affected at the deeper level of our being. He gives the example of our having a collection of theories that can be misused in clinical work to falsely reassure us of having an expertise.

Bion's emphasis on the defensive nature of 'knowing-about' however might obscure other healthier and demanding relations to knowing. At the time of writing the paper, I had become aware, in relation to a patient, that both she and I knew more than we were really taking ownership of. I had also been noticing afresh Bion's strikingly assertive announcements of what he knew. This is most evident in his 'Theory of Thinking' paper: a minimalist statement of his model of the mind., as well as his statement on psychoanalytic technique in his 'Memory and Desire' paper. In this chapter, I will focus on 'Theory of Thinking'.

Bion's two minimalist papers reminded me of another piece of writing I had come across as a philosophy student some years ago: Ludwig Wittgenstein's *Tractatus Logico-Philosophicus* (1921). In the *Tractatus*, Wittgenstein presents a series of propositions that he believed were all there needed to be known about the mind (from a philosophical viewpoint). The publication ends with the well-known statement: 'Whereof one cannot speak, thereof one must be silent'; everything that could be said about the mind Wittgenstein thought he had now articulated.

Wittgenstein later became critical of the *Tractatus* and went on to write a much more exploratory book, *Philosophical Investigations*. This work has characteristics in common with Bion's own more exploratory writings (which contrast to his 'Theory of Thinking' and 'Memory and Desire' papers). I began to wonder whether putting the two men's work together might throw more light on Bion's relation to what he knew.

So, by this stage in formulating the paper, I had the following three points:

- On the patient and I going further into what we respectively knew: I will give some background and clinical material from two sessions to attempt to illustrate what I mean by this, but essentially it involved taking the focus off the relationship between us and putting it on to each of our relations to ourselves.
- Bion – and Wittgenstein's – minimalist assertive statements of what they knew: Bion's 'Theory of Thinking' and Wittgenstein's *Tractatus*. Wittgenstein became critical of his *Tractatus*. Bion, I think, always had a place for austere models (of mind, of technique) that stated what he had learned in a way that would provide an unequivocal instrument for use in his and other's explorations.
- A question: might these austere, assertive statements have played a significant role in the preparation for the much more explorative journeys then taken by both men? The much more exploratory work of both men in which we see them both go more deeply in to where they are (instead of finding an 'objective' position from which they can view the whole scene). This does involve going into the unknown, but it also involves going more deeply into what is already known. This sounds rather abstract I know, but I hope to flesh it out below.

Some background to Bion's 'Theory of Thinking' and Wittgenstein's *Tractatus*

Both texts were written somewhat outside the traditional institutional context.

Through the 1950s, Bion was working in the Klein group. Then in the late 50s/early 60s he became more independent of the group and more independent of the psychoanalytic establishment generally. He stopped writing papers for the congresses and publication in the *International Journal of Psychoanalysis*, and started writing in his own format (the four books of the 60s). Bion wrote the 'Theory of Thinking' paper on the cusp of this change. It is the last of his papers for a congress and publication, but is also very different to the ones that preceded it. It is a statement of Bion's own model of the mind. Originally published in the *International Journal of Psychoanalysis* with the title 'The Psycho-Analytic Study of Thinking', this paper, just nine pages long, is still one of the ten most frequently accessed articles in psychoanalytic literature.

Turning now to Wittgenstein. In 1911, Wittgenstein, originally from Vienna, arrived at the University of Cambridge to study philosophy with

Bertrand Russell. However, it was while serving in the Austro-Hungarian army during World War One and then as a prisoner of war in Italy that he wrote *Tractatus*. A significant philosophical text of the twentieth century, the *Tractatus* was taken up by the logical positivists (see Wittgenstein's response to this below) and it is highly thought of more generally in relation to systematic philosophizing.

Some shared characteristics of Bion's 'Theory of Thinking' and Wittgenstein's *Tractatus*

To my knowledge Bion's 'Theory of Thinking' contains no question marks. Wittgenstein's *Tractatus* does, but they are questions he has already answered and function to introduce what he already knows.

Both pieces have numbered paragraphs, although Wittgenstein's involves a more complex numbering system. This formatting denotes the significance of each point and the importance of grasping them individually.

Both pieces of writing are pared back to the central points being made – they are short and minimalist in style.

Both pieces also convey a sense of strenuously standing up to a negative force. For Bion, the negative force is death instinct functioning/the evacuation of experience. In Wittgenstein's *Tractatus*, the adversary is all the philosophy that has come before him.

Both pieces of writing are forceful statements that the writer is introducing a new and comprehensive view.

Bion's later work and Wittgenstein's *Philosophical Investigations* (1953)

I remember being struck as a philosophy student by Wittgenstein's description in *Philosophical Investigations* of how we come to see something new. This happening, not by following an inductive or deductive path, but an 'all at once' reorientation, rather like what we describe in psychoanalysis as the identification of a selected fact (see the Endnotes section at the end of this chapter):

> The problems are solved, not by giving new information, but by arranging what we have known since long.
> (Wittgenstein, *Philosophical Investigations*, 1953)

When one studies philosophy – as some of you will know – it tends to be taught in terms of what an individual mind (Plato, Aristotle, Descartes, Hume, Kant) has been able to think. Many years ago, while a philosophy student, I was in the bookshop across the road from my university when I came across a book by Bion, who I hadn't heard of before. The book was

Learning from Experience. I was struck by Bion's view that the human mind develops through the mind of another. The infant's mind develops through the mind of the mother and parents. The nature of this early development would surely mean that the adult mind operates somewhat differently to how I was being taught: a model of each mind building itself. I began to read Bion and ended up a psychoanalyst!

Meanwhile, in *Philosophical Investigations*, Wittgenstein argues that we think only in a shared language and that there is no such thing as a private one.

Are Bion and Wittgenstein actually thinking differently themselves in these works, as well as coming to new conclusions about the nature of thought? Interestingly, both men's later work has received similar criticism. Here is a critique of Wittgenstein's *Philosophical Investigations* by the British philosopher A.C. Grayling:

> It is vatic [prophetic], oracular; it consists in short remarks intended to remedy, remind, disabuse. This gives the later writings a patchwork appearance. Often the connections between remarks are unclear. There is a superabundance of metaphor and parable; there are hints, rhetorical questions, pregnant hyphenations; there is a great deal of repetition. Much of this is deliberate...for Wittgenstein's style is expressly designed to promote his therapeutic objective as against the 'error' of theorizing. Few, however, would seriously recommend this way of doing philosophy to, say, students. Wittgenstein's method, in the wrong hands, provides excellent cover for charlatanism, since it is intended to avoid system and with it the required clarity, rigour, and accuracy which theoretical work demands and which philosophers in general seek.
>
> (Grayling, 1988 p. 132)

Here is the psychoanalyst Edna O'Shaughnessy talking about Bion's later work:

> ...Bion's thinking becomes less disciplined, and his language then begins to suffer the defects of its qualities. By 'less disciplined', I mean mixing and blurring categories of discourse, embracing contradictions, and sliding between ideas rather than linking them. These features are apparent, indeed intentional...
>
> In 'Dreams and Occultism', Freud observed how 'when life takes us under its strict discipline, a resistance stirs within us against the relentlessness and monotony of the laws of thought and against the demands of reality testing. Reason becomes the enemy' (1933, p. 33). Contradictions have their appeal: breaking the laws of thought and reason brings a quantum of verbal fun. Yet, in scientific writings, such transgressions lead us to anything and everything we fancy ...
>
> (O'Shaughnessy, 2005, p. 1524)

What these critiques seem to be missing is an appreciation of how both men now see themselves as making approaches into unknown territory. In both Bion and Wittgenstein's new models, understanding can be gleaned in varying ways, from varying perspectives, however, it is not possible to 'objectively' have sight of everything in a comprehensive way.

Wittgenstein's critique of his earlier theory is convincingly seen in his response to the attention given to his *Tractatus* by the logical positivist circle in Vienna:

> Soon after it [the *Tractatus*] was published, Wittgenstein suffered a crisis of faith in its ideas....
>
> Meanwhile, the logical positivist circle in Vienna read the Tractatus and were enormously inspired. They invited Wittgenstein for a research visit in 1927. He came, but refused to answer any questions about his book, stating that he could no longer understand the thinking of someone who would write such stupid things. Instead, Wittgenstein sat with his back to his audience reciting poems by Indian mystic Rabindranath Tagore.
>
> The logical positivists were not amused. They nevertheless adopted a host of Tractatarian ideas.
>
> (Legg, 2022)

One of the key characteristics of both men's more exploratory work is the sense of their going further into where they are. No longer is there believed to be a point where they can stand and come to a comprehensive objective view of the working of the mind. They are in it: in the pathways laid down in their relationship with others, in the partial views and varying perspectives, in the intention to explore and clarify different ways of 'knowing'. Both had a remarkable gift in finding out about the detail and depth of where they were.

A Clinical Illustration and Bion's Concept of 'Suffering'

In this second part of the chapter I am going to talk about some clinical work in which I came to think that both I and the patient needed to go further into what we each respectively knew already. This is not a defensive 'knowing about', but a kind of knowing that involves taking on the weight of owning/being responsible for what one knows. Bion calls this 'suffering' what one knows.

The material is from a long analysis at a frequency of four times weekly. The patient is an artist in her 30s who sells her work through a gallery. She lives and works in an artist's collective.

Over time the patient and I were slowly able to make more helpful contact in sessions. However, at the end of each session, and particularly during breaks, something happened to her which left her disorganized and empty. She felt completely defenceless in the face of this.

We also seemed at cross purposes talking about her early life, with her wanting to talk about the damage she'd experienced, and my feeling cautious about this, and that I was being manoeuvred to take sides. I found it hard to get a feel for where she was.

Over time I came to think that the 'cross-purposes' was not just a temporary lack of understanding, but a subtle, long running argument. When I put this to the patient, she agreed (implying that she had long thought this). There were also management issues, where I was not able to accommodate what she would have chosen, and this put an additional strain on the existing dynamic. While we had now identified the argument, it seemed fearfully difficult to do anything about it. The argument went like this:

The Patient's View

If I knew how disastrously empty the patient was left feeling, how could I end the session or take breaks? The patient surmised I must be either weak minded (allowing myself to *not* know) or cruel (take pleasure in it). I was responsible for the terrible experience she was having.

My View

What was happening at the end of sessions and breaks that meant the patient was left without an internal link to me and our work? Was she somewhere so enraged at coming up against a 'no' from me that she evacuated the work done in the session? My view made *her* responsible.

It was helpful when together we put into words that she wanted me to experience her as a baby. Babies can't be left, there is no issue about oedipal boundaries, babies just can't be left. Behind this, there was a sense of her having been traumatized as a baby. Were the boundaries of analysis re-traumatizing her? Although she wanted me to experience her as a baby, it didn't seem possible to be in contact with the traumatized baby her. Did this put us in an impossible position? We certainly seemed stuck.

In a recent session we both, at different points and in different associative contexts, referred to a baby being left on a hillside. I remember thinking of Oedipus, the baby on the hillside, but was unusually dismissing it at the same time. This is ongoing work and I would hope to return to this with her, but for our discussion now, what about our associations to the baby on the hillside? Oedipus as an innocent baby abandoned by his parents (her view of what I'm doing), or Oedipus as a danger to the parents (my view of her not wanting the boundaries of analysis).

Were we in a desperate situation or actually an ordinary analysis being made dramatic? This was a recognizable problem for the patient more generally.

I was aware of a difficulty in having enough separateness myself to have a view that encompassed us both. I could do this at one level, but I strongly suspected I wasn't doing it deeply enough. I did, however, have moments of becoming more able to, one in particular. I was half asleep in my bed and more able to think! I don't usually consciously take my work to bed and the very fact of this may have been a symptom of my difficulty properly taking it all in. However, I suspected in this context I felt safe enough to let *in to* my mind what I actually already knew.

I had been struggling in this analysis in relation to guilt. The patient tried to make me feel guilty. I tried to keep an eye on what I might actually be guilty of. My half-dream thought was that I was holding off the guilt and I should let myself feel it. This came as a relief and I felt better rooted in the analytic position again. A second, I suspect related, change around the same time was that I found myself wanting to say to the patient 'do you really not know more about ...' whatever we were talking about (at times in quite a repetitive way). Could I help her go further in to what she may know already? I began to talk more frankly to the patient about the extent to which she may be censoring what she said to me – and what she said to herself. The patient had long believed that she had to manage me to prevent me leaving. This, she said, was why she had to censor what she said. She continued: 'it would be freeing if I didn't have to do this', this said with feeling, and with some surprise. Now, not so inhibited by my own guilt, I was more able to ask (myself) why I couldn't be more in contact with her distress. Also, why was she so worried that I was constantly wanting to leave? Looking more closely in a recent session, with her telling me more too, I could see that she made a subtle attack and then told me about her distress. I might previously have underestimated its effect on my ability to take in her distress. We needed to get hold of the attack and her distress at the same time, instead of splitting them between us as an argument.

Some Detail on Bion's Use of the Term 'Suffering'

Bion's main discussion of 'suffering' is in his chapter on 'Medicine as a Model' in *Attention and Interpretation* (1970). Here he notes that whilst in medicine disease should be recognized by the physician, in psychoanalysis recognition – knowing – must be by the 'sufferer' too.

> There are patients whose contact with reality presents most difficulty when that reality is their own mental state. For example, a baby discovers its hand; it might as well have discovered its stomach-ache, or its feeling of dread or anxiety, or mental pain. In most ordinary personalities this is true, but people exist who are so intolerant of pain or frustration (or in whom pain or frustration is so intolerable) that they feel the pain but will not suffer it, and so cannot be said to discover it. What it is that

they will not suffer or discover we have to conjecture from what we learn from patients who do allow themselves to suffer. The patient who will not suffer pain fails to 'suffer' pleasure and this denies him the encouragement he might otherwise receive from accidental or intrinsic relief.

(Bion 2019, pp. 227–228)

'Suffering' involves discovering something – and discovering it as belonging to oneself. It strengthens the self. Patients can be exposed to frustration and pain by the very structure of analysis including the end of sessions. 'Suffering' the end of a session may involve the person discovering that they are someone who feels frustration/pain/anger when what they are involved in is taken away. 'Feeling' frustration and pain would, by contrast, be experienced as pain and frustration being cruelly inflicted on the patient by the analyst and not holding any information for the person about themselves.

In relation to the analysis above, the patient intended that I should feel guilt. As I have said – I intended that I should hold it off! By contrast, when I was more able to 'suffer' the guilt I quite quickly located the guilt that did belong to me. What I would call 'ordinary guilt' – that which is just part of being an analyst. The patient likewise was holding off her own knowledge of how she moved 'sideways' away from our work. This at the cost of depleting her sense of self.

Concluding Thoughts

My title is 'On Going Further into What We Know'. I *haven't* wanted to talk about Bion's questioning of the defensive use of knowledge. I *have* wanted to talk about his going further into what he knows:

- in his austere statements in his 'Theory of Thinking',
- going more deeply into where he is in the present moment in his more exploratory work
- in 'suffering' what is known

Is there a link between these three modes of knowing? When I looked at the version of this chapter I gave at the conference I thought I was trying to overly push them together. In this version I decided to go into what I thought about each mode and to see what came of that. One link I have made is a possible alternation in Bion's work between gathering together what he knew (on the mind, on technique), stating it as austerely and forcefully as possible and using it as one of his instruments in his journeys into the unknown. Secondly, the fact that 'suffering' is addressed in his later work may indicate a deepening interest in our relation to what we know – a relation that involves ownership (at the level of our being) and responsibility. This would apply to knowledge held with austere authority or more explorative modes.

In some of his later seminars, Bion comments that we work hard for what we know. It isn't to be used defensively, but neither is it to be taken lightly. He takes on the task of going further into what he knows. This is happening in his work at the same time as the exploration of what isn't known and the identification of what can't be known.

End notes

Selected fact

What Henri Poincaré calls a selected fact is a 'condensed' fact that profoundly orientates us in relation to the myriad things happening.

> Bion: Poincaré describes the process of creation of a mathematical formulation thus:
> Bion quoting Poincaré:
> If a new result is to have any value, it must unite elements long since known, but till then scattered and seemingly foreign to each other, and suddenly introduce order where the appearance of disorder reigned. Then it enables us to see at a glance each of these elements in the place it occupies in the whole. Not only is the new fact valuable on its own account, but it alone gives a value to the old facts it unites. Our mind is frail as our senses are; it would lose itself in the complexity of the world if that complexity were not harmonious; like the short-sighted, it would only see the details, and would be obliged to forget each of these details before examining the next, because it would be incapable of taking in the whole. The only facts worthy of our attention are those which introduce order into this complexity and so make it accessible to us.
> (Poincaré, 1914)
>
> Bion: This description closely resembles the psychoanalytic theory of paranoid-schizoid and depressive positions adumbrated by Mrs. Klein. I have used the term 'selected fact' to describe that which the psychoanalyst must experience in the process of synthesis.
> (Bion 2019, p. 339)

Bion and Wittgenstein

Bion makes reference to Wittgenstein's work in *Philosophical Investigations* in his 1955 paper on *Language and the Schizophrenic*:

> Wittgenstein (Philosophical Investigations) has deprecated this view [Augustinian theory] and seems to me to put forward a theory which is

both more comprehensive and more realistic. In ordinary speech the meaning of any given word, and still more the meaning of the sum total of what a man says, depends upon the synthesis of a complex variety of elements; sounds have to be combined to form words, and words, sentences.

(Bion 2019, p. 80)

Bion is referring to Wittgenstein's view that speaking a language is part of an activity or life form – a 'language game'. The meaning of a word is based on how the word is understood in the 'language game'.

Although Bion to my knowledge does not go further into Wittgenstein's work, others have looked in depth at links between the work of the two men, including psychoanalyst Dr. James Ogilvie.

References

Bion, W. R. (1962). The Psycho-Analytic Study of Thinking. *International Journal of Psychoanalysis* 43: 306–310. Also in: Volume VI *The Complete Works of W.R. Bion* (2014) (CWB) with the title 'A Theory of Thinking'.

Bion, W.R. (1962). *Learning from Experience.* London: William Heinemann Medical Books. Reprinted in 1984 by Karnac Books. Also in: Volume IV CWB.

Bion, W.R. (1967). 'Notes on Memory and Desire', *Psychoanalytic Forum*, 2(3).

Bion, W.R. (1970). *Attention and Interpretation.* London: Tavistock.

Bion, W.R. (2019). *The Complete Works of W.R Bion*, Vol. IV. Ed. by C. Mawson. Abingdon: Routledge.

Grayling, A.C. (1988). *Wittgenstein: A Very Short Introduction.* Oxford: Oxford University Press.

Legg, C. (2022). The Conversation. *Scroll-in.* Jul 15, 11:30 pm.

O'Shaughnessy, E. (2005) Whose Bion? *International Journal of Psychoanalysis* 86: 1523–1528.

Poincaré, H. (1914). *Science and Method.* New York: Dover Publications.

Wittgenstein, L. (1921). *Tractatus Logico-Philosophicus.* First edition in English, London: Kegan Paul, 1922.

Wittgenstein, L. (1953). *Philosophical Investigations*, translated by G. E. M. Anscombe. Oxford: Basil Blackwell.

Chapter 4

Dreaming, Day-dreaming and Sensing Things Together

Peter Goldberg

Dreams and dreaming have always had a special place in psychoanalysis. It is true that in certain epochs and in some schools of analysis, interest in the function of dreams and in dream interpretation became less prominent; yet in their case reports, analysts of every persuasion seem to have remained in love with dreams. The way analysts thought about dreams was always more or less the way that Freud thought about dreams – until Bion, who extended Freud's dream model by bringing attention to the fact that dreaming is not built in, and cannot simply be counted on in analysis, but is a capacity, along with thinking, that must be gifted intergenerationally from caretakers to infant, and a lot can go wrong in this transmission. To account for instances where the capacity for dreaming is faulty, or fails altogether, Bion (1962) brought to bear his conception of Alpha Function. This led to the proposal that the psychical work of dreaming occurs not just when we are asleep; that the night dream is just one manifestation, a phenotype of a more general function of the mind, that Bion would eventually refer to as *dream-work-alpha*. In other words, insofar as this generic dream-work capacity is up and running, we are unconsciously engaged in dream activity all of the time, day and night.

Bion's expansion of Freud's dream theory into a full-blown theory of mental functioning has been most fruitful in its effects on modern analytic thought and practice, revolutionizing our view of how the analyst works, highlighting the role of reverie and the centrality of intuition in the analyst's work. Here the analyst is re-imagined as a dream-worker, and – in the hands of post-Bionian writers – as a collaborative dream-worker, insofar as the clinical situation is viewed more fully intersubjectively as a shared dream space.

This elevation of the oneiric activity of the mind to perhaps the central function in mental life does raise a question about our conception of what analysis does: Should we consider access to the dreaming function of the mind the essential aim – perhaps even the *sine qua non* – of analysis? If so, what is entailed in the cultivation of the oneiric capacity? Is it the analyst's alpha function alone that cultivates this capacity where it is lacking in the patient, or does the dream function depend upon some other essential kinds of collaborative mental functioning between analyst and patient? In other words, does the oneiric dimension define the work of analysis, or constitute just one aspect of the analytic process?

To investigate this question, I will look at two phenomena – firstly day-dreaming, and secondly the place of sensory experience (what Bion designated in terms of beta elements) – to ascertain the degree to which these phenomena depend on the oneiric or dream function of the mind to attain psychical significance, or whether in fact or the work of day-dreaming and of sensory experience are psychical functions in their own right, complimentary to the oneiric dimension of the mind.

Day-dreaming

Day-dreaming has received relatively little conceptual attention in psychoanalysis, perhaps because, being more under the aegis of consciousness and thus more affected by censorship and secondary-process organization, day-dreams seem unlikely to offer the kind of access to the repressed unconscious that dreams do. Being dream-like, day-dreams might seem naturally to be products of the oneiric dimension of the mind, merely a particular form of dreaming. Upon closer inspection, however, might there be something distinctive about the way day-dreams work?

There are a number of ways in which we day-dream, ranging from passive to active: On one hand, we think of it as something like absent-mindedness or distraction, something one falls in to. On the other hand, there are more intentional, even ritualistic ways in which we might transport ourselves into day-dreaming. But whether one slips into it or actively seeks it out, to day-dream is to suspend time and enter temporarily into an altered state of imaginative conjecture, removed from the immediate demands of everyday life and from relational demands. As such, an important and positive role can be recognized for day-dreaming: In contrast to defensive dissociation, where there is an attempt to escape one's feeling-self by going somewhere else in one's mind, day-dreaming allows us to generate new ways of feeling one's way into things, of imaginatively re-creating oneself-in-the-world.

Yet because day-dreaming affords a precious opportunity for imaginative elaboration of self-experience, a place to go for re-creation, it also naturally lends itself to transient defensive uses, but can be deployed also as a means to escape more compulsively into alter-worlds. Just as it can be an incomparable source of creative consolation, day-dreaming in its negative iteration can become too much of an alternative place to live, an irresistible retreat, and a prison house of addictive distraction.

Day-dream in Relation to Other Modes of Thought

For the purposes of this discussion, it is worth differentiating day-dreaming-proper from other types of waking imagery. We retain an awareness of reality while day-dreaming, which distinguishes it rather obviously from hallucination and from flashbacks, where judgement and the sense of what is real are disabled. But day-dreaming differs also from the everyday spontaneous occurrence of dream-like thoughts and images, the spontaneous appearance in consciousness of fantasy (often dismissed or quickly repressed) that arrive unbidden, often dystonically, dystonic in a way that day-dreaming is not. Day-dreaming is always to some degree an invited experience, a more structured mental activity, one that takes time and a particular kind of concentration.

Day-dreaming differs as well from the kind of thinking and imagining that orients us – along the lines of thought as trial action – towards some specific task in the external or internal worlds. Day-dreaming is essentially pointless: Its goal is nothing other than to achieve a day-dream state. It is an end in itself. Indeed, if a day-dream begins to be more task-oriented, it begins to lose its day-dream quality, giving way to other types of mental process (problem solving, drive discharge, anxiety management, defensive control, etc.).

Day-dreaming and the Drives

Day-dreaming, like dreaming itself, is fueled by unconscious wishes, but the function of day-dreaming cannot be reduced to sublimation of the drives, in the Freudian sense of diverting the sexual instincts away from their aim and into sublimatory channels of drive satisfaction. Clearly the daydream state carries its own kind of erotism and pleasure. The aim of day-dreaming is not simply drive-management, but entails something more complex, something closer to an imaginative, exploratory search for a pleasurable way of being in the world. In this regard, the day-dream state carries its own kind of erotism and pleasure. All of this puts the function of day-dreaming closer to Winnicott's description of creative apperception, of discovering a viable sense of psycho-somatic aliveness. In other words, day-dreaming is a state in which desire is procured or re-invented, not extinguished through gratification (cf. Laplanche, 1997).

Dreaming and Day-dreaming

I have briefly indicated some of the features that distinguish day-dreams from other kinds of waking imagery. Now I would like to turn more directly to the question of how day-dreaming differs from dreaming-while-asleep. Do they differ substantially? Might it not be parsimonious, in light of Bion's expansive concept of dream-work-alpha, simply to say that day-dreaming is a particular manifestation of the oneiric function of the mind, a conscious counterpart to dreaming during sleep, serving an essentially similar dream-work purpose? Or is day-dreaming doing something quite different? Might it even constitute a substantially different psychical operation?

There can be no doubt that day-dreams possess oneiric qualities, that they do perform dream-work – which, of course, is why we call it *day-dreaming*. Day-dreams involve pre-conscious negotiations and transformations into alpha elements, just as dreams do: i.e. in both dream and day-dream the repressed makes its way through displacement and disguise and compromise formation into a *mise-en-scène* acceptable to consciousness. Yet the two phenomena seem designed for different purposes. The most obvious difference is that we are more conscious of the process of day-dreaming as it happens, whereas the process of dreaming is entirely unconscious; only the manifest dream becomes conscious. Day-dreaming often takes the form of a kind of story-creation, following the conventions of narrative construction and secondary-process logic. Unlike fantasy and dream, day-dreams have to make some kind of sense. Does this simply mean, because it is more under the control of consciousness, that day-dreaming is a kind of dreaming-lite a poor cousin to real dreaming in the realm of mental life, hence unfit to serve as the royal road to the unconscious? Or is there more to it?

From a certain point of view, dreaming and day-dreaming can look quite opposed. If we accept for the moment my initial premise, namely that day-dreaming is an essential psychical activity in its own right, and that furthermore it seeks nothing outside itself – that achieving the day-dream state is its own satisfaction – then we seem to be confronted with something that seems quite at odds with Bion's conception of dream work. After all, what lies at the heart of Bion's conception of dream-work-alpha is his recognition of the reality-principle function of dreaming – that the dream work not only affords wish-fulfillment, as Freud described, but effects realistic psychical and real-world transformations. This would seem to place day-dreaming, with its indifference to realistic transformations, in a quite opposite camp, perhaps aligned entirely with the pleasure principle. But day-dreaming has its own reality principle orientation, probing the possibilities of new ways of living in reality.

This brings us to what is perhaps the most distinctive thing that day-dreaming does, namely the way in which it affects a shift in locus of attention, an alteration from one state of consciousness to another. In other words, in addition to working to some degree like a dream (i.e. employing dream-work functions), day-dreaming also involves the use of hypnoid mechanisms, comparable to what we see in distraction, in hypnotic and trance states, in auto-suggestion and mesmerization – mechanisms that work at the level of attention and alterations of consciousness. Indeed, this shift in attention and consciousness would seem to be an essential feature: day-dreaming gets us away from one state of perception into another, from attention to reality into an imaginative mode. In learning to day-dream, we learn the skill of intentionally inducing altered states. Might we view this aspect of day-dreaming as a psychical function in its own right – something like *day-dream-work* – that exists alongside the dream-work function of the mind? Is day-dreaming how we learn to transit from one state to another in a way that is personal and elective rather than imposed?

Day-dreaming, Play and Illusion

In outlining some of the ways that the function of day-dreaming differs from that of dreaming, it is worth noting that, for all its distinctiveness, day-dreaming does not stand apart but, in fact, shares a great deal with – and even epitomizes – an entire sphere of psychical states that are essential to a meaningful life: The particular effect of day-dreaming, whereby a temporary state of altered consciousness is established along with its own special kind of pleasure, is very much like what occurs in other domains of everyday experience – when a child begins to get absorbed in play, for example, or when we listen to a story, get lost in a book or in a concert performance or theatrical production. Each of these activities invokes imaginative states that have no realistic goal beyond the experience of being transported into an alter-world for a period of time. While any of these experiences might provide fodder for subsequent dreams or evoke dream thoughts, the actual state of attention, concentration and immersion in these activities is more akin to day-dreaming. There seems to be a fundamental human striving to gain access to these day-dream-like states, perhaps because they offer the possibility of new ways of experiencing the external and internal worlds, of tapping into ways of being beyond the limits of the self.

From this perspective, the ability to transition into day-dream states begins to look like it is part of a distinctive type of mental function that plays a special role in our sense of personal realness and our ability to participate in and make use of cultural and collective domains.

Being in the analytic situation itself would seem to share some important characteristics of day-dream-like states (re-creational states like story-telling, music-listening, reading, playing, as well as participating in cultural activities). The analytic setting affords the patient (and analyst) an opportunity to enter an altered state of consciousness, a state (whether we describe it in terms of free-association, transference, therapeutic regression) that is not itself oriented towards problem solving in the world, nor wedded to any particular task, beyond effecting this peculiar analytic state of mind for a certain amount of time.

Bion (1970) himself was emphatic about the importance, in analysis, of putting aside the desire for a particular outcome or effect or cure. The libidinal situation in analysis likewise emulates the erotics of daydream-like states, where the aim is not sexual fulfillment per-se, but the development of a personal ecology of desire. Perhaps we can say that what analysis specifically does is nothing other than induce an analytic state of mind, allowing access to what Bion (1970) referred to as the *psychoanalytic function* of the mind. The conclusion I draw is that the analytic process depends not just on the activation of dream-work functions, but on what I am calling *day-dream-work*.

Day-dreaming as Portal into Collective Experience

We tend to think of day-dreaming as a private and solitary experience, but paradoxically the ability to enter a day-dreaming state depends upon the workings of what Winnicott (1960) called a "facilitating environment". Just as dreaming proper requires that the individual's being able to enter a state of sleep, day-dreaming, too, requires environmental conditions that keep impingements at bay and allow the play of imagination. The ability to have a solitary day-dream derives from the experience of having been helped into day-dreaming. Here we might find an analogy with Bion's incomparable insight that our own capacity for thinking and dreaming was gifted us by others; this seems equally true of day-dreaming.

In the first place we were day-dreamed into existence by our parents and care-givers, and we learned to day-dream in their presence and under their tutelage.

Cultivation of the capacity for day-dreaming may be considered vital to discovering a personal way of being in the world. While dreaming is the epitome of the spontaneous individual creative work of the mind, day-dreaming leads us naturally into collective domains of the imagination, providing a natural portal of entry into culturally-constructed alter-worlds of all kinds – of storytelling, fable, communal activities of recreation, ritual worship and celebration. All of these work to temporarily transcend the boundaries of individual perception, tapping into the individual's own capacity for day-dreaming.

All cultures cater extensively to the need to be transported through day-dreaming, providing venues where the private re-imagining of self is elaborated through the auspices of cultural production. In this way, the individual is recruited into cultural experience: We become acculturated as we learn to make use of the available amenities that will help take us in and out of day-dream states. Much will depend, then, on what may be called transformational aesthetics – on what is available in the immediate cultural, group and family environment – to allow and facilitate day-dreaming.

It may have occurred to you already Winnicott's (1971) conception of the transitional area and potential space, as epitomized by the activity of play, overlaps with my description of day-dreaming; indeed his distinction between phantasying and imagining precisely captures the contrast I have drawn between day-dreaming and other spontaneous kinds of waking imagery. Perhaps most pertinent is his description of how play involves a pleasure that is interrupted by gratification of the drive. Since day-dreaming primes the individual for entry into alter-worlds, we can see how readily day-dream-work can be appropriated by virtual realities – social-media platforms, internet gaming, fan fiction, virtual relationships – that have rapidly emerged as cultural domains defining self-experience.

I will venture the following: Whereas dream-work entails the unconscious search for individual drive-satisfaction and individual psychical transformations, day-dream-work tackles problems of one's social nature – the personal, imaginative search for ways of being amongst others, of finding one's place in the world. Whether it is practiced as a solitary activity or in group or communal settings, day-dreaming is a way of imagining oneself into new kinds of life activities, and there is a distinct kind of pleasure in this.

Dysfunction in Day-dream-work

Sponsored by the social, economic, and familial cultures we live in, day-dream-work affords opportunities for personal experimentation with how to be in the world. But where the immediate milieu fails to secure opportunities for daydreaming, the potential for a personal sense of creative engagement with the world is compromised: what Winnicott (1971) described as transitional experience is impaired. The result is an excessive demand to attend either to external reality or to psychic reality. Here daydreaming tends to lose its transient imaginative quality and, instead, on the one hand, will mutate into a compulsory or even addictive defensive activity of the mind that must be held onto and never relinquished. Used in this way as a defensive retreat, day-dreaming tends to repeat and reinforce familiar, repetitive scenarios (along the lines of what Winnicott called *fantasying*). Here day-dreaming loses its elective, transient qualities, instead becoming fixed and habitual (along the lines of what Winnicott called *fantasying*), and in this way takes on the character of a fetish. The compulsive day-dreamer finds themselves trapped in a cocoon of persistent make-belief: Lacking the improvisational and playful quality of normal day-dreaming, the capacity for imagination is recruited instead to keep the isolated individual visiting the identical day-dream scenarios, in an inescapable repetition. On the other hand, the very ability to day-dream may be forfeited and lost, leaving the individual without the possibility of imagining themselves into life. The inability to make proper use of daydream states is a common feature of contemporary maladies.

Day-dream-work in Analysis: The Framing Function and Induction into an Imaginative State of Mind

The dream-work approach bequeathed us by Bion places as the highest value – in fact insists upon – the analyst's ability to participate in unconscious communication so as to generate new alpha elements. But to the extent that what I have called *day-dream-work* plays a significant part in psychic life, what are the implications for clinical work?

It is evident that having a night-time dream requires that one is already in a dream-ready state, which at minimum entails being asleep. If we set aside this minimum requirement by saying, as Bion does, that a kind of dreaming goes on all the time, even when awake, then it makes sense to assume that the analyst, and possibly also the patient, will be *dream-ready* at the outset of the session – that the potential for alpha function transformations is already present in the field (i.e. even if the patient lacks alpha function, the analyst is potentially able to provide it). But what if some other process is required to make the clinical field dream-ready?

The work of analysis depends upon the patient undergoing a particular shift in attention, as they enter the office (or log onto a video app), a transient change in consciousness – something akin to a dream-ready state – befitting the work of analysis (freer movement of thought and reflection, deeper perceptiveness of emotional states). We ourselves must undergo a similar transition at the start of every hour, a broadening and loosening of consciousness, while being more-or-less attuned to the patient's shifts in state. In this way, there takes place a mutual induction into an altered state of perception, close to what I have described as a day-dream-like state, where the self can be re-imagined. This conception of analysis portrays not so much a process of unearthing hidden causes than an ontological process of expanding self-experience (Ogden, 2019).

Of course this shift in consciousness does not happen automatically in every case, and in some instances the inability to transition into an analytic state of mind becomes the central feature of the treatment. This requires, whether we are aware of it or not, a shift in attention to the task of searching for, or building, a viable way of sensing things together.

Normally the ability of analyst and patient to sync up and shift into a heightened state of perception depends on the ongoing background function of the frame. Whatever it's other important purposes (professional, ethical, social, symbolic, economic), the frame is indispensable in its function of focalizing a specialized kind of attention and perception, framing a specific configuration of space/time, which the analyst oversees and invites the patient to enter, thereby ushering the patient into (and then out of) an analytic state of mind, a state that makes possible something closer to dreaming, e.g. the so-called free associative state.

Bleger (1967) described the frame as a mute backdrop or non-process that nevertheless sometimes moves to the foreground of analysis when primitive symbiotic or psychotic elements are activated. This background activity of framing allows what Civitarese (2021) refers to as the fictional world of analysis – the "characters in the field" – to emerge in the foreground. But this framing activity is far from passive or static: It relies on constant activity at the level of a sensory symbiosis formed between analyst and patient, prompted by shifts and improvisations in prosody of our speech, in tone, tempo and rhythm and pace of psycho-sensory activity. Insofar as it allows the participants to transition together into different states of consciousness, framing is the essential embodied activity underwriting symbolic communications in the analytic encounter, and day-dream-work provides a model for this.

If we look beyond the analytic situation, we will see the framing function at work as a transitory device operating in a wide range of individual and cultural activities that engage the imagination. (Consider what happens as the lights go down at the start of a theater performance, the rituals undertaken in preparation for sleep, or the special place in the house where a child must go in order to play or daydream.) It seems to me that entering the analytic session is analogous to the transition that occurs when we shift into a daydream state, insofar as it engages an imaginative mode of mental functioning, one that involves an expansion of consciousness into the external and internal worlds.

Failure to Day-dream

Where transiting between states is impaired or blocked, the resulting clinical picture invariably includes some mixture of narcissistic vulnerability, rigid forms of self-containment, omnipotence, ritualistic self-regulation, fear of new experience and change, and inability to learn from experience. Perhaps most crippling in these cases of what might be called *failure to day-dream* is the resulting foreclosure of access to *shared* psycho-sensory and affective states, those states of communal perception where we are not simply our individual selves any longer, where the limitations imposed by the individual ego are temporarily set aside, allowing for the expansion of consciousness to include within its scope new ways of experiencing self and world.

These states of expanded consciousness are commonly described and accounted for in terms of religious or spiritual experience, while in psychoanalysis Bion's (1970) conception of "O" provides a psychical model for trans-individual experience of unison. I think we may also view the trans-individual dimension of experience as arising from the collective nature of sensory perception – the transpersonal sources of how we sense and perceive things.

Where the individual is unable to enter transiently into these shared sensory states, the result is a particular kind of isolation, life in a psycho-sensory cocoon, shut out of the sensory commons (Goldberg, 2012), hence unable to partake of the cultural storehouse which provides us ways of being embodied in the world. This *failure to day-dream* is implicated in a range of clinical pathologies that we see everywhere these days – disorders of attention, of sensory integration, compulsive and autistic regimes of self-regulation, psycho-somatic dissociative states, all of which reflect intolerance of changes in state. These are not so much disorders of thought as of embodied fellow-feeling, disorders of sensory orientation in the world.

For many patients who lack the ability to transition from one state to another, the analytic setting itself becomes the site of restoration of a capacity for shared psycho-sensory experience. Now the analyst's work shifts to actively procuring a shared framework of experience and perception, which involves joining the patient at the psycho-sensory level, which underwrites the individual's imaginative capacities.

The Beta Function

Turning now from the question of day-dreaming, I would like to look briefly at sensory experience with a view to its relation to the dream-work functions of the mind. I have already suggested the importance of the transitional rituals, or what may described as the inductive function of the analyst – the way the analyst invites the patient into a shared state of sensory perception, much as a conductor does through bodily gestures and the motion of the baton. This vital dimension of what goes on in analysis would seem to entail something other than alpha function transformations of sense data, as Bion described it, but a process of engagement at the level sensory experience itself. How might we conceptualize this type of shared psychosensory activity?

We are all familiar with Bion's (1962) model describing how sensory experience (beta elements) are transformed into *alpha elements* in order to be worked on psychically. In his focus on the un-nameable psychical thing in itself, Bion remained a sceptic of the ways our senses join us to the world and each other. He felt sensory experience misleads us by trapping us in the record of the past, or the illusion of the future (memory and desire), thus robbing us of experiential analytic access to psychical reality (O). Though he did not theorize a place for sensory experience itself as a part of psychic life, there are hints in Bion's work that he recognized the significance of the function of beta elements beyond being simply raw material awaiting transformation into alpha elements, or as disintegration products or debris where alpha function has failed. Indeed, Bion's description of the operation of a *beta screen* in psychotic conditions hints at a type of psychical mechanism organized on the basis of beta elements alone, albeit one that stands in the way of the development of thinking and dreaming. But should we exclude the possibility that beta elements have a properly psychical role to play, and are crucially organized in their own right?

I have thought that the concept of Alpha function should not exclude the possible existence of something like a *Beta function* – something that organizes sensory experience in a non-verbal pattern language that we all learn and that requires no translation into verbal symbolic language. Yes, Alpha function transforms beta elements into verbal symbolic form suitable for thinking and abstraction and explicit communication, but our psycho-sensory experience hums along in highly elaborate pathways of perception and fellow feeling, without needing such transformation at all. Music is perhaps the most obvious evidence of this, but it is evident everywhere, in the prosody of our speech, in activities like throwing and catching a ball, laughter and idle conversation – the ways in which we move together in the world.

This is largely where we live, woven into a fabric of communal psycho-sensory life, where a vital part of psychical meaning is sourced and generated.

Without access to this shared, trans-individual domain of shared existence, we are left isolated, with only our idiosyncratic dreams and fetishes to console us. Psychoanalysts today are searching for ways to broaden clinical theory to take into account how we live in the fabric of shared feeling and sensation, and how the analytic situation is, amongst other things, a site of re-creation of links to the collective and cultural contexts. Bion's conception of O can be viewed as a premonition of this paradigmatic development (although here I am thinking of a type of O that involves shared sensation).

Our Present Maladies

It is hard to begin to get the measure, in our current era, of the degree to which isolation from communal life and the diminishment of everyday shared embodied rituals has contributed to the proliferation of disorders of attention, of self-regulation, of OCD…. Today we are surrounded by sensory disorders of many kinds, along with prevalent anxieties of depersonalization and disembodiment. Do these primarily reflect defective Alpha function, or are our modern maladies more a matter of failures and impediments in what I call Beta function? Suffering minds today are often those that have lost mooring in the shared patterns of embodied living in the world, have become disenchanted and alienated from the sensory commons.[1] Certainly these problems occupy center stage in my work with people in their 20s and 30s, who show marked deficiencies in their ability to navigate daily transitions in state, or to access and make use of collective embodied forms of experience.

Note

1 For the purposes of the current discussion, is it possible that impairment of day-dream-work, and corresponding disabling of dream-readiness, might sometimes actually hyper-activate the oneiric functions, throwing the patient into a manic attempt to produce meaning while being bereft of access to an imaginative capacity? These are the patients whose speech is empty, as Lacan put it, or who remain locked at the level of false self-organization (this may overlap with Bion's concepts of reversal of perspective, negative k). Where the analytic setting fails to aid in transitioning, might it become itself the scene of a futile search by the patient for meaning, where the oneiric itself is perverted towards hypermentation?

References

Bion, W. (1962). *Learning from Experience*. London: Tavistock.
Bion, W. (1970). *Attention and Interpretation*. New York: Basic Books.
Bion, W. (1992). *Cogitations*. London: Karnac.
Bleger, J. (1967). Psychoanalysis of the psychoanalytic frame. *International Journal of Psycho-Analysis*, 48: 511–519.
Civitarese, G. (2021). The limits of interpretation. A reading of Bion's "On Arrogance". *Int. J. Psych-An*. doi:10.1080/00207578.2020.1827954.
Goldberg, P. (2012). Active perception and the search for sensory symbiosis. *Journal of the American Psychoanalytic Association*, 60: 791–812.
Laplanche, J. (1997). The theory of seduction and the problem of the other. *Int. J. Psych-An*. 78: 653–666.
Ogden, T.H. (2019). Ontological Psychoanalysis or "What Do You Want to Be When You Grow Up?", *The Psychoanalytic Quarterly*, 88: 4, 661–684.
Winnicott, D.W. (1960). The theory of the parent-infant relationship. In *The Maturational Processes and the Facilitating Environment*. London: Hogarth Press, 1965, pp. 37–55.
Winnicott, D.W. (1971). *Playing and Reality*. London: Tavistock.

Chapter 5

We-ness and Bion's Psychoanalytic Function of Intuition[1]

Giuseppe Civitarese

Over time, I have become more and more convinced that Bion's thought represents the grafting of his theory of group psychology onto Kleinian psychoanalysis. This hypothesis helps me clarify how and why Bion increasingly shifts the latter toward the former, even if, to some extent, he gives the impression that he does so without really being aware of it.

In Bion, this gaze brought to the truth of what *is* happening in the present becomes extreme. In fact, he himself presents his contribution as a way of improving the precision of observation in psychoanalysis.

But how does Bion improve observation of the "facts" of analysis—for him, essentially the emotional experience?

He does so in various ways, and I would like to emphasize at least three: (a) if to peer into the depths of the inner world, the Kleinian analyst uses the optical microscope of early Oedipus and the processes of splitting and projective identification, Bion uses the electronic microscope of a new theory of thought; (b) he elaborates the concepts of *transformation* and *intuition*; and (c) as I have alluded to in my title, he gradually replaces the perspective of the subject with that of the *we* or the *intersubject*—a shift, however, that is only fully achieved in post-Bionian analytic field theory (FT).

Here I briefly address only points (b) and (c).

Intuition Versus Insight

The concept of *transformation*, so central to Bion, is in contrast to that used by Freud of *distortion*, and the former is meant to focus all eyes on what *is* happening here and now in the session. But his insistence on the concept of *intuition* is also something that deserves the greatest attention—especially, I would say, because it acts as a handmaiden to that of *transformation*.

Intuition should serve as a way to "see" the transformations of the unconscious emotional experience in the session—setting aside the search for causes in the past. On the reasons for implementing this exclusion, Bion (1977) is crystal clear: "We can do nothing about the past" (p. 47). The idea of the past must not hinder the observation of what takes place before the eyes of analyst and patient.

Through intuition, the analyst can monitor dynamic changes in the quality of psychic and interpsychic ties and consciously try to influence them. One can see why, for Bion and even more so in FT, intuition assumes the absolute importance we are familiar with.

It should be said at once that his concept of *intuition* does not correspond precisely to the sense that we give to this word in everyday language. Despite shared etymologies, which would have them perfectly equivalent, *intuition* is different from *insight*. While the latter is close to the idea of coming to possess knowledge about a given object, intuition is here to be understood, rather, as a specific psychoanalytic concept that expresses a function: it is the *capacity* to intuit.

Bion never ceases to reiterate that this capacity is acquired through exercise and discipline. The analyst, he writes, "has to 'intuit'"; if she cannot do so, she had better go back to analysis or change her profession. Intuition, then, is not the opposite of technique; rather, it is *to make oneself such a master of technique as to make it invisible.*

But let us try to specify the nature of intuition more precisely.

If intuition is something that can lead to insight but is not insight proper, it means that, compared to the latter (which is more abstract), it is closer to the (affective, bodily) pole of sensoriality and imagination.

As a specific psychoanalytic concept, the essence of intuition lies mainly in the aptitude to *visualize images* or *pictographs*. Paraphrasing Rimbaud (1966, p. 307), one could say that the analyst has the capacity to intuit when, through a "rational derangement of all the senses," she succeeds in becoming a "seer." Paradoxically, she is someone who can *see* facts unrelated to the immediate experience of seeing with the senses—or who, from sensory input, can extract essences.

Essentially, it amounts to knowing how to make use of *reverie, hallucinosis*, and *dream*.

But what, then, are the exercises to develop this ability?

First of all, what is needed is to have adequate theoretical preconceptions about the unconscious processes of the psyche and the meaning of dreaming. For the subject, dreaming is the function deputed not to conceal, but to be a kind of breath of the psyche, to constantly create meaning for emotional experience. If this is not taken into account, given that we are always dreaming, even in wakefulness (a fact), it becomes impossible to grasp the principles of Bion and FT (Bionian field theory).

Second, it is essential to learn how to use the so-often-misunderstood technique of negative capability/faith (NC/F; see Civitarese, 2019).

Listening without memory or understanding does not mean looking at objects in the field of observation and giving up *any* kind of memory or understanding. That would be absurd and unworkable. Instead, listening without memory simply means to stop looking at objects in the field as factual events or concrete objects; in other words, it means *to temporarily give up the realistic view we use in everyday life.*

Why? Because in the perspective of speculative thinking and psychoanalysis, this is a naive and fallacious view, even if appropriate for certain contexts.

The exercise is to *actively* familiarize ourselves with this mode of vision to the point that we can forget it and let it present itself to us as though from outside.

If the analyst listens in this way, subtracting the veneer of concreteness that hides the dream behind the effect of reality (Barthes, 1982), then she reads all phenomena of the dream spectrum as texts of the unconscious and as a psychoanalytic function of personality.

We-ness

I now come to point (c), which is the most difficult and counterintuitive: to see the unconscious-as-a-function (which I have just mentioned) not as peculiar to the individual, but as a group or field function, so as to broaden the range of intuition.

For me, what is at stake in attempting this is to further refine the metapsychology and technique of FT. Emphasizing the shift from the *you* or the *you/I* to the *we* is a way of making it easier to work within the perspective of the analytic field.

Of what does the shift from the *you/I* to the *we* consist?

I have already expressed my view that in bringing his revolution to fruition, the deep inspiration of Bion's thought is to come to see the analysand/analyst pair as a small group composed of two people (Civitarese, 2021a). It follows that the analyst has the task of raising the problem of what is, so to speak, the *basic assumption*, instant by instant, that is governing its functioning: whether or not it is conducive to the psychic growth of both the group itself and of each of its members (Civitarese, 2020, 2021b).

If we postulate that from the meeting of the patient's and analyst's unconscious, a third (relational, communal) unconscious is created, it follows that what the analyst intuitively sees has to do not only with the patient or the analyst separately, but virtually with both—or rather, that it is *co-created*. The viewpoint of *we* as surpassing the relational viewpoint of *you/I* (in which, compared to classical psychoanalysis, the analyst is already more willing to consider her own unconscious participation in the processes of analysis) enhances the significance of intuition, elicits more data from it, and *allows for hypotheses to be formulated that otherwise could not be made.*

The Rigid Teacher

When the *we* perspective replaces the relational *you/I* perspective, it happens, for example, that the analyst has to conjecture that an emotion attributed only to the patient is also unconsciously her own, and vice versa.

Let me give an example. Mario tells his analyst about a kindergarten teacher whom he hated because she was cold and rigid. We infer that this may not only be a trauma from Mario's past and try to understand it as such: that is, not only is it a distorted view of the analyst-as-severe-teacher, and not only does it pertain to Mario's unconscious but adequate view of the analyst. In addition, emotions and feelings of anger and frustration recounted through the teacher-character are *simultaneously* both Mario's and the analyst's; they express the quality of their emotional link in a given moment.

Listening in this way, the analyst would be forced to realize that, *really,* perhaps the climate of the treatment is intoxicated by mutual anger and aggression.

Taken to the limit, assuming responsibility for the "rigid teacher" would also be possible for the analyst, following the (relational) hypothesis that it might be an unconscious but adequate (not distorted) representation that Mario has of her. However, this would remain a split representation. We would still be within a perspective of *suspicious listening*, even if self-directed. The therapist would still miss the fact that she is not only the aggressor, but also—symmetrically—the victim.

Sta sü de Doss[2]

Lucio comes to the session like a poodle that never stands still. He takes off his shoes, rests his feet on the couch, and begins trying to "extort" personal information from the analyst. The analyst thinks that he tends to shorten the distance too much. She struggles not to answer questions but feels annoyed, intimidated by the patient's stuffy manner. Transference? Projective identification? Enactment? All legitimate theoretical angles, but all remaining within the frame of *you* or *you/I*.

From the point of view of the *we*, it would be: "(Perhaps) *we* tend to shorten the distance too much." To obtain additional data, the analyst could question the potentially equally stifling significance of, for example, her own seemingly benevolent and welcoming way of trying to establish a climate of intimacy for the patient.

Lucio would indeed seem to have suffered in the past from a primary relationship in which he was emotionally "aborted" at birth, and in which the object proved to be stifling or imminent (Lacan, 2004), but the question becomes whether and how the two are *now* functioning as a couple in *Medea* mode, so to speak. Behind apparent overfamiliarity lies, perhaps, the deficit of recognition that, according to Bion, may lead to nameless terror.

What, then, might be an alternative attitude on the part of the analyst? For example, the analyst might choose to work more on the level of nonverbal communication of emotions and affects—even just naming them, simply but pointedly.

My impression is that, although not in a clear and distinct way, Bion comes to bend the principle of self-interpreting-through-dreaming as a way of coming to exist as subjects in a gradually more intersubjective or field direction.

I specify that I now use the term intersubjectivity not to indicate the interaction between separate subjects, but as an index of what they have in common—that is, to indicate their dimension of co-belonging or mutual implication (Civitarese, 2021c). No longer do we see the unconscious as a psychoanalytic function of the patient's or analyst's personality, but rather as a joint psychoanalytic function. We no longer view the patient or analyst as the dreamer who is dreaming the session, but rather the group of two as the dreamer.

I was saying, however, that as far as I know, Bion seems to pursue this direction, but only "obscurely." On the one hand, his emphasis on the O of the session—which on a practical level, I can translate only as the basic assumption of the dynamic patient-analyst system—and on the fact that, by definition, emotion always has to do with the relationship, leads one to think that he is reinventing individual psychoanalysis in terms of group psychoanalysis. But on the other hand, in his published vignettes, Bion continues to work as a Kleinian who interprets to the patient his/her excessive envy.

The group inspiration of his more mature thinking is not yet fully made explicit, either theoretically or technically. This is a source of endless misunderstandings—for example, about his alleged mysticism, etc.

It is here, in my view, that FT (field theory) intervenes. Faithful to Bion, his spirit, and many of his concepts, it is also true that at the same time, it is original and goes beyond Bion. At the very least, if we think about how we can work with Bion today, FT frees his thought once and for all from the residual ties to Kleinian psychoanalysis, which for many is still the way to read him and be inspired by him.

In a way that we do not find systematized at all in Bion, FT transposes his absolute and "outrageous" concentration on intuition—that is, seeing that which in itself is not of the order of phenomena that can be perceived by the senses, and develops tools that are suitable for the purpose, but above all is versatile and easily transmissible.

All these instruments have the characteristic of dimming the lights of sensory perception to bring out the much weaker but valuable lights of hallucinosis. By *hallucinosis*, I mean the almost literal ability to dream while awake. *Literal* because until we wake up, we do not know that we are dreaming. In this sense, analysis is the art of hallucinosis and surprise (or creative and felicitous shock).[3]

Even transformation into dreaming, which Ferro recommends, should be used by making it part of NC/F (negative capability/faith), that is, by forgetting about it. When it resurfaces as a guest that was not expected, it takes on the quality of hallucinosis.

Grasping this principle as in itself paradoxical *(be aware that everything is [also] a dream, but at the same time, forget it—in the extreme, keep it only as unconscious memory)* also serves to allay the anxiety of those who would aspire to use the FT vertex in clinical work, but who find it "too difficult." It would suffice to think that it is true that everything can be seen as a dream, but that this being all-dream most of the time may well remain in a virtual state and not be *intentionally* actualized (although this can and should be done, if necessary), and that instead it becomes actualized when the theory itself comes back as in a dream.

Normally, on the other hand, for much of the session, the dream understood as the possibility of deconcretizing reality remains in the background (virtual) and only occasionally becomes actual (I mean when reality, or better the narrative of reality, is deconcretized). To know how to pause in reality as the virtuality of the unactualized dream is to know how to make double use of NC/F. It amounts to knowing how to use it not only to bracket concrete reality, but also to dodge as much as possible the risk of reifying theory itself.

In fact, it is obvious that if the analyst always aspired to be as aware as possible of the dream dimension of the session (in other words, if she obsessively questions the unconscious meaning of every detail of the analytic conversation), she would end up suffering from a kind of "over-attention disorder." This would no longer be dreaming, but a kind of *psychotic dreaming*—that is, without really being able to either sleep or stay awake. Instead, in Rubin's bistable or ambiguous figure, which I take as a metaphor for a binocular view on the facts of analysis, the oscillation from the profiles of two separate subjects to the vase of what is shared should ideally catch the analyst as if by surprise.

But this will never happen unless the analyst has long and actively practiced the skill of intuition, that is, the ability to "see" the phantasmagorical images of the dream. The pianist will never develop the talent to play as spontaneously as possible unless he has studied technique so well that he can do without it.

It is true that, as long as we remain within a given perspective, we must be consistent. This means that, in principle, oneiric intuition, translation into fiction, and deconcretization will be capable of pertaining to *absolutely everything—even what some analysts, who also speak of third and thirdness, "automatically" relegate to the register of the patient's historical or material reality.*

The other implication is that if I am not so concerned about transforming into a dream, the conversation can proceed supported by reality, and also on the reality of the more traditional theories of psychoanalysis; in this way, the analyst also gets to know the "profiles" well.

We see that what is at stake is the possibility of going beyond the relational model. The intuitive "vision" from the analyst, the moment she lets the unconscious memory of theory and technique work within her (assuming, of course, that they are *already there* somewhere), is what we call *reverie*. This can be visual, olfactory, tactile, kinesthetic, acted, etc., but also ideational. By *ideational reverie*, I mean a reverie that is not in the form of an image, but in the form of a thought. This thought, however, would have the quality neither of a cold logical deduction with respect to the events of the analysis nor that of mere association. Rather, it would be at first glance a dream-thought.

Given what it is called to do, which is to foster the psychic growth of the patient, there will always remain a hierarchy between reality (outer world) and dream (inner world), in favor of the latter. At the same time, I don't see why we should disavow the wisdom that psychoanalysis has accumulated over more than a century. Keeping something in the background does not mean erasing it. On the contrary, it is the opposite, because what is in the background contributes meaning to what is in the foreground and vice versa.

A Straitjacket

Olga had been destined by her mother to be perfect in everything. *At one point, I have an image of her imprisoned in a straitjacket.* With amazement, I realize that I have represented to myself iconoclastically not only the extreme state of helplessness from which Olga suffers and that has somehow been imposed on her, *but also that this situation has produced in her a "psychosis" and a state of great "psychomotor agitation,"* as of one who needs to be physically contained.

My intuition allows me in a lightning-fast manner to represent to myself in an effective sensory and emotional form a drama that I could have, yes, coldly hypothesized, using my knowledge of psychopathology, but that certainly would not have allowed me to stand as "close" to Olga's emotional experience.

Here again, the next (and for me, the decisive) step would be to ask whether, using the perspective of the *we*, the same figure of the straitjacket might not reflect a particular emotional climate or quality of bonding in the care or basic assumption of the small group-to-two. Psychosis at this point would be our "psychosis."

Concluding Comments

In my view, to *intuition* in Bion and FT, we should assign a *specific* meaning—it should not mean an idea that is simply brilliant and to effect, but that is more or less obscurely unclear as to where it comes from, or that is not in some way traceable to a reverie or transformation into a dream or into hallucinosis.

Otherwise, in what way could intuition be "disciplined"? What could exercise to enhance the analyst's capacity for intuition possibly consist of?

Such interventions, which are sometimes brought up as examples of intuition in Bion's sense, have the air of arbitrary, when not outlandish, interpretations. Lacan (quoted in Wilson, 2020) would rightly say that they "contribute to increasing the 'vacuous buzzword of intuitionist'" (p. 111).

Perhaps we understand a little better why Freud (1955) distrusts intuition, which he likens to divination and revelation, and which in essence he sees as irrational, and quietly rubrics "among illusions, among the gratifications of impulses of desire" (p. 263).

In my opinion, we should not superficially dismiss Freud's doubts. That is why, in this chapter, I have tried to subtract intuition from readings that instead make it something excessively vague and undefined and redefine it as the analyst's capacity to get in touch with the spectrum of the oneiric.

My other point is that it is preferable to see intuition as not belonging to one or the other, but as a joint, intersubjective, or field event. With FT, the surprising point of view is always that of the *we*. The consequences are varied and remarkable in various ways. The one I have focused on here is precisely to broaden the scope of intuition as perhaps the analyst's main tool. When seen from the angle of the *we*, intuition comes to illuminate hitherto unseen aspects of the analyst's unconscious participation in the treatment process.

In this way, intuition brings *vitality* to the analytic process; it is in itself therapeutic because it demonstrates confidence in the unconscious ability of the couple (and thus of each) to transform the emotional experience. Finally, it helps the analyst avoid making guilt-ridden interpretations.

Notes

1 This paper was presented at the International Bion Conference "Oneiric Dimensions of the Mind" in Mexico City, November 10–13, 2022, and is about to be published in *Fort Da*.
2 This expression in the dialect of Pavia could be translated as "Don't stay on me".
3 This is not unlike Baudelaire, who elaborates a theory of the function of *shock* in poetic creation. The shock sought by the artist is the way that he chooses to awaken a slumbering sensibility, to generate a jolt of vitality, to initiate a process of psychic "digestion" that is crucially not limited to the appropriation of consciousness (and of voluntary memory, with which it is identified), but that also calls for the putting together of corporeality and affects (life). It is a shock that is potentially not unpleasant, but "happy," like those we seek in aesthetic experience. On this, see Benjamin (1955).

References

Barthes, R. (1982). *L'Obvie et l'obtus: Essais critiques*, III. Seuil.
Benjamin, W. (1955). The storyteller. In D. J. Hale (Ed.), *The novel: an anthology of criticism and theory, 1900–2000*. Blackwell Publishing, 2006.
Bion, W. R. (1977). *Two papers: The grid and caesura*. Karnac, 1989.

Civitarese, G. (2019). On Bion's concepts of negative capacity and faith. *The Psychoanalytic Quarterly*, 88, 751–783.
Civitarese, G. (2020). Regression in the analytic field. *Revue Roumaine de Psychanalyse*, 13, 17–41.
Civitarese, G. (2021a). Experiences in groups as a key to "late" Bion. *International Journal of Psychoanalysis*, 102, 1071–1096.
Civitarese, G. (2021b). Bion's graph of "In Search of Existence." *American Journal of Psychoanalysis*, 81, 326–350.
Civitarese, G. (2021c). Intersubjectivity and the analytic field. *Journal of the American Psychoanalytic Association*, 69, 853–894.
Freud, S. (1955). New introductory lectures on psycho-analysis. In J. Strachey (Ed. & Trans.), *The standard edition of the complete psychological works of Sigmund Freud* (Vol. 12, pp. 1–182). Hogarth Press. (Original work published 1932)
Lacan, J. (2004). *Anxiety: The seminar of Jacques Lacan, book* X. A. R. Price (Trans.). Polity, 2016.
Rimbaud, A. (1966). *Complete works, selected letters*. W. Fowlie, Trans. University of Chicago Press.
Wilson, M. (2020). *The analyst's desire: The ethical foundation of clinical practice*. Bloomsbury Academic.

Chapter 6

"To Risk Sailing Westward to Cathay and Thence Safely Home"[1]

Oneiric States of Mind

Avner Bergstein

I would like to begin with a rather long quotation from Meltzer, in which he describes his experience of participating in Bion's seminars. He writes:

> When confronted with a direct question, Bion's tactics seemed military indeed. He seemed to start off in a direction quite contrary to that of the question, as if in retreat from the aggressive intent, then made a wide sweep, ending by taking the enemy, not even on its flank, but from the rear.[2] During this excursion he would make little sallies at the question, trying one vertex after another, until one of them found a rather soft spot in the armour of the language in which the question had been phrased. But I also noted times at which I lost the thread of his excursion and was left indignant, having more than half forgotten the question, even when it was one of my own. During the course of those excursions that I did succeed in following, I thought that I could discern a certain sequence to his probings. He seemed often first to tap the wording to see if the vocabulary of the question rang true or seemed soft at the center. Then he probed it for preconceptions, leading qualities, various penumbra of meaning from common parlance. Then often came a kind of brutal thumping of its presumption that an answer existed as the *"malheur de la question"*. And finally, he attacked it as a problem related to the central question of the meaning of psychoanalysis as a thing-in-itself. Because of this method, certain phrases central to his modes of thought, certain analogies and metaphors turned up again and again, giving a superficial impression of repetitiveness, cliché, covert confusion, or even boredom. But that was the impression when one had lost the thread of the excursion. When one was able to hold on to the thread, the performance was rather dazzling, though not always immediately illuminating.
>
> (Meltzer, 1980, pp. 470–1)

"Now that is a rather military model of Bion's mentality", Meltzer goes on to say,

> but one can discern the voyager in mental space-time convinced that the world of the mind is four-dimensional and infinite. Recklessly he surges on, depending on the center of gravity of his fundamental sanity holding him in orbit so that he can **risk sailing westward to Cathay and thence safely home**. So, I am suggesting that *the diameter of his circle* was a measure of his confidence in his sanity, which allowed him to abandon himself with such startling freedom to the capacity of his mind for imaginative conjecture.
>
> (1980, pp. 470–1, emphasis added)

This, I suggest, is a beautiful description of the oneiric state of mind, highlighting the mind's capacity for perpetual movement in its quest for truthfully apprehending reality.

Francesca Bion (1997) too draws attention to Bion's very discursive, almost conversational style, which might be thought of as rambling; but that it is in itself a good example of the "large circumference", since *return to the theme at the end* is notably enriched by all that has occurred "on the way".

The ultimate reality of the session – *in transit*

When patient and analyst meet, there is some kind of ultimate reality there – the *evolving* analytic session itself. This is O, beginning with the experience at the very outset of the session, or even before…with all the infinite emotions, sensations, external stimuli, internal stimuli, all interconnected and intermingled in an infinitely complex mesh of relationships. And since it is infinite, it is unknowable in its entirety. We can only **approach** its innumerable, different facets, at any specific moment, and even then, only partially. As Bion (1964) says, when one starts a session with a patient it is dark, it is formless, it is a void. It is a potentiality of all the distinctions that have not yet been made.

As elaborated elsewhere (Bergstein, 2025), O is ultimate. There is no "analyst's O" or "patient's O", **only O**, which is the unknowable, ever-changing *and*, paradoxically, irreducible ultimate reality **of the session** – which is one for patient and analyst. O is not *any* emotional experience in reality or in the patient's life, as that would make analysis of that experience impossible since it is inaccessible to the analyst. As Bion (1965) will say, "any O not common to analyst and analysand alike…may be ignored as irrelevant to psychoanalysis" (pp 48–49). It is thus the infinitely interconnected experience itself, as yet unrepresented in patient's *or* analyst's mind. Bion is concerned with observation of *the evolution*, or *the transformation* of the emotional experience, in the immediacy of the here and now of the session, and it is that which he will want to interpret and help the patient get in touch with.

That is the reality present in the session. Only that *evolving* experience is available to both patient and analyst and is experience-near. Hence it might be apprehended and not only talked *about*.

What Bion is concerned with are the *processes* by which the patient transforms the experience to achieve *their* representation of it, and the *processes* by which the analyst does so.

But there's the difficulty. Because these very processes too, are in constant transit and transformation, forever influencing and transforming each other. "What makes the venture of analysis difficult", Bion says, "is that one constantly changing personality talks to another" (1977a, p. 47). The mind is not just a passive repository of memories, emotions, conflicts, deprivations, defenses and ways of coping to be revealed. Rather, the mind is *a process*, infinite in its essence, invariant and ultimate and *at the same time* in perpetual evolution, expansion, and transformation.

For Bion, as for Freud, getting in touch with reality, and expanding our capacity to be in touch with reality, *is* what matters. That is the work of analysis, and that, to my mind, is the motive for working in the immediacy of the "here and now" – not only as a method for uncovering early memories, or for repeating, remembering and working through – but rather for being **in** the ever-changing, elusive and illusive present, **in** reality, and try, as closely as possible, and yet always fail, to be in contact with this reality in its unending transformations. And this reality is external **and** internal, sensuous **and** psychic, conscious **and** unconscious, to name just a few possible vertices of the *infinite* vertices from which one can "observe" the multidimensional, ultimate reality of the session.

Hence, at heart, reality can never be known. We can encounter, at best, and then only momentarily, its fragmented representations dispersed in space-time, often deformed beyond recognition. Over hundreds of hours of analysis, we may stumble upon fragmented bits of experience, accumulating over time. No individual instance is illuminating in itself, but the *invariance* becomes apparent through the perpetual movement between different vertices, and when these experiences are repeated over time; and then, only if they are seen to form part of a coherent whole (recall the well-known "I scream" vignette).

An oneiric state of mind is thus one in which *the diameter of the circle* is large enough, allowing for the continuous movement between different vertices. This is reminiscent of the notion, stated by Peirce, that truth is the unattainable goal of a never-ending process of inquiry (in Hustwit, 2007). Thus

> any attempt to classify the material with which we have to deal should be regarded as provisional, or transitive; that is to say, part of a process

from one thought or idea or position to another – not a permanency, not a halting spot at which the investigation is ended... The analyst's role...is one which inevitably involves the use of transitive ideas or ideas in transit.

(Bion 1977a, pp. 43–44)

*

I would like to approach this view of reality, very briefly, from two more vertices – Process Philosophy and the Jewish mystical tradition. The fact that different disciplines, at different times and from different vertices describe the same experience enables a "multi-ocular" view, affording a sense of truth.
"**All things are in flow...**"

Some insights from Process Philosophy

Whitehead's Process Philosophy seems to have inspired Bion's thinking about psychoanalysis enormously (cf. Torres 2013). I will only touch on some points of affinity between the two, in reference to both thinkers' depiction of reality.

Process Philosophy argues that the language of development and change are more appropriate descriptors of reality than the language of static being. This tradition has roots in the pre-Socratic Heraclitus who likened the structure of reality to the element of fire, *as change is reality and stability is illusion.*

Furthermore, Whitehead (1925) notes that the human intuitions of science, aesthetics, ethics, and religion each make a positive contribution to the worldview of a community. Yet in each historical period, any one or combination of these intuitions may receive emphasis and thus influence the dominant worldview. As described by Hustwit (2007), it is a peculiar characteristic of the last centuries that scientific pursuits have come to dominate the worldview of Western minds. For this reason, Whitehead seeks to establish a comprehensive descriptive theory of the world, that aspires to do justice to the *various* human intuitions and not only the scientific ones. Toward this end, Whitehead argues that philosophy's task is to synthesize, scrutinize and make coherent the divergent intuitions gained through ethical, aesthetic, religious, and scientific experience (Hustwit, 2007). This is of course reminiscent of Bion's notion that a sense of truth is experienced if the psychoanalytic object is viewed from different vertices (i.e. scientific, aesthetic, religious, mathematical, artistic, etc.), and the conjunction of these views confirms that the object experienced by different emotions is the same object.

Process Philosophy as a whole employs three methodologies, usually simultaneously: empiricism (knowledge from experience), rationalism (knowledge from deduction), and speculation (knowledge from imagination). Whitehead's famous metaphor for philosophy, so similar to Meltzer's description of Bion's mentality, is that of a short airplane flight. Philosophy begins on the ground with the concrete reality of lived experience. Experience provides us with the raw data for our theories. Then, our thought takes off, losing contact with the ground and soaring into heights of imaginative speculation. During speculation, we use rational criteria and imagination to synthesize facts into a (relatively) systematic worldview. *In the end, however, our theories must eventually land and once again make contact with the ground – our speculations and hypotheses must ultimately answer once again to the authority of experience.* By taking this airplane flight as a model for speculative metaphysics, Whitehead envisions the process of metaphysics to consist in an unending series of 'test flights', as our metaphysical conclusions are never final and always hypothetical (Hustwit, 2007).

In a similar vein, Bion too is concerned with the capacity to apprehend reality *in transit*, perpetually moving between different phenomenological derivatives of this evolving ultimate reality, between its realization and abstraction. It is a paradoxical state of mind founded on the Heraclitean assertion that "No man ever steps in the same river twice, for it is not the same river and he is not the same man". And yet, we might add, at the same time they are. Therefore, *transformations and invariance* are at the foundation of Bion's thinking about psychoanalytic observation. The patient we see tomorrow is not the one we saw today, and yet, at the same time, they are. All things are in flow, and at the same time, paradoxically, absolute truth, the "poppishness", is invariant.

A view from the Jewish mystical tradition

The notion of ultimate reality *in perpetual transit* lies at the essence of the Jewish mystical tradition's depiction of the Godhead. In the Biblical account of the story of the Burning Bush, God is described as calling out to Moses from a bush that was on fire and yet was not consumed by the flames. The text portrays Yahweh as telling Moses that he is sending him to the Pharaoh in order to bring the Israelites out of Egypt. Yahweh tells Moses to tell the elders of the Israelites that Yahweh would lead them into the land of "milk and honey".

Dov Elbaum (2016), a scholar of Kabbalah, maintains that the flaming fire is not only the medium through which God reveals himself, but rather, the fire, *in its very essence*, contains the message that is to be conveyed. One reason why the fire captures and hypnotizes our gaze is the innumerable, infinite forms it takes, its countless, unpredictable and ever-changing guises, a classical chaotic structure (like reality). In fact, we have, in this vision, an invariant bush and a perpetually transforming fire.

Moses is at first reluctant to take on the role of leadership and asks "When I come to the Israelites and say to them, 'The God of your fathers has sent me to you,' and they ask me, 'What is His name?' what shall I say to them?" (Ex 3:13). The voice of God emerges from the flames and replies: *ehyeh ašer ehyeh*, meaning "I shall be that I shall be", (in the *future* tense and not as often cited "I am that I am").

As Elbaum (2016) writes, emerging from the flames, these words acquire a simple, and yet fascinating depiction of the Godhead, of Ultimate Reality: "I am like the fire, I am the eternal freedom *to become* in any imaginable form; the possibilities are infinite. I am always becoming, in perpetual transience. If I shall determine who I am or allow you to determine me in your consciousness, I shall miss the very profound essence of my being".

"I shall be that I shall be" is a God that identifies itself as a dynamic, eternally ever-changing being, forever becoming, forever evolving, and it is this evolution that defines it.

Moreover, the word we often pronounce as Yahweh, or Yehovah, is in effect unpronounceable in its original Hebrew. Nowhere in the Bible is it written with any vowels and its pronunciation is unknowable. Any definitive pronunciation renders its dynamic essence static, and in that sense, amounts to turning away from its reality. By the same token, the dictum in Jewish religion that one cannot utter God's name, is from a Kabbalistic point of view, not because it is forbidden, but because *it is ineffable*. It is literally unsayable. Unknowable!

Again, the affinity to Bion's thinking about ultimate reality, O, is evident.

I am reminded of the story of the Burning Bush since, remarkably, Bion alludes to this very Biblical story a number of times in his semi-fictional *A Memoir of the Future*, where it is the woman (often personified in the characters of Rosemary and Alice), veiled and full of awe, who is unknowable. And the woman, perpetually transforming, is asked over and over again (alluding to the biblical story of the Burning Bush) "Who are you?", for which countless words are thrown back: "I am what I am. I am God. I am Satan. I am hell fire. I am the burning bush. I am the fire that all men worship. I am Satan…I am the dreamer…" (Bion 1975, p. 36) and on and on over three pages. Strikingly, Bion intuited these same thoughts about the infinite, multi-dimensional, transient ultimate reality.

This perpetual movement is tantamount to psychic aliveness, to *emotion*ality (originating, in fact, from the word *motion*), and is that which facilitates the never-ending journey towards a truthful apprehension of reality.

For Bion, psychoanalysis aims not so much at facilitating the transformation of unconscious into conscious, but rather facilitating the movement between finite and infinite (Bion, 1965). *It is not arriving at THE meaning that is at the core of psychoanalytic work, but rather the perpetual pursuit in search of infinite meanings*, akin to the infinite forms taken by the flaming fire. Hence, being in contact with reality requires a mind capable of tolerating the complexity and the painful and unsettling, unending *evolution* entailed in this encounter.

The Diameter of the Circle

The circle and its diameter serve as a model for the mind (Bion, 1963, 1977b, 1965, 1975). If we realize that mental space is vast, then we understand that it can accommodate a vast number of possibilities. Since mental space is infinite, *anything* can be thought! In external reality, however awful, there are limits to what can happen because they are governed by the laws of nature. But, if we allow ourselves to have contact with *psychic* reality, there's no limit at all to what can happen. *Anything*, however awful, *can* happen in a dream (Bion, 1967).

We are then in a domain that has no finite boundaries and must adapt our method of inquiry accordingly. Since reality is infinite and in perpetual transit, *a mind of a large diameter ultimately affords a more truthful apprehension of this reality.*

A large enough diameter is thus conductive to the development of thought and personality, allowing for unpredictable and fascinating discoveries. However, at the same time, as often cited by Bion, "The eternal silence of these infinite spaces terrifies me" ("Le silence eternel de ces espaces infinis m'effraie") (Pascal, 1669). Consequently, we witness the reduction of the fruitful, growth-producing thought of a large enough diameter, by the successive diminutions of diameter, until it becomes a sterile argument, of which the diameter is further diminished until the circle itself disappears and only a point remains. The individual then, patient or analyst, may have unquestionable certainty in their argument which has become ossified and static, and hence, they may have no doubt of their (hallucinated) sanity. Conversely, if the diameter gets wider, then the individual becomes aware that there might be two or more dissimilar, perhaps contradictory, views about the same facts, which might then be accompanied by a feeling of frustration, confusion, emotional turbulence and even madness. If "madness" is feared, the argument must be of small diameter to prevent the conjunction of meaning and a feeling of madness (Bion, 1963). This is, again, illustrated in one of the classic tales from the Jewish mystical tradition.

The Talmudic tale of the four sages who entered the "Orchard" (*Pardes* in Hebrew, denoting the divine secrets of the Torah) is a fascinating and foundational story about four Jewish sages, namely Ben Azzai, Ben Zuma, Elisha ben Abuyah (known as the "Other One") and Rabbi Akiva (The Talmud, Tractate *Hagiga* 14b). It is a parable and an allegory for becoming at one with the Godhead, which has been given numerous interpretations by various scholars over the years, and to which I cannot do justice in this short depiction. In brief, it is the tale of three of the four who met with disaster following their inquiry into the unknowable and the hidden secrets of the Torah, and only one who came out unscathed.

The Orchard they enter – the firmament of the heavens – is built like a magnificent palace. The pure marble of which the palace is built is so smooth and shiny that it might appear to be spring water. Yet this, as Rabbi Akiva warns, is an illusion. Anyone who enters must be able to identify the real material that the stones are made of from their illusive appearance, for fear that they be physically harmed. The parallel lesson seems to be a warning that one is approaching a place where they will be faced with an illusion that truth is known and clear. However, one must pause and delve into the truth albeit without drowning in this illusion. Seeing the illusion as truth itself is the greatest danger in the mysterious world of the Torah.

The tale of the four sages can be seen to represent the spectrum of theologically acceptable and unacceptable ways of using creative imagination to envision the paradoxical relationship between the incorporeal God of Judaism and its self-manifestations in theophanic forms perceptible to human beings (Subtelny, 2004).

It is told that Ben Azzai peered and died. Ben Azzai was a Chassid and a great scholar; however, he was so engrossed in his atonement, believing he could truly see God – an experience too overwhelming for his soul to endure. His death seems to hint at God's words "For no man shall see me and live" (Exodus 33:20).

Ben Zuma peered and lost his mind. Although recognized in the Talmud as one of the great sages of his generation, he was still quite young. As such, his capacity for spiritual absorption was more limited. The overwhelming brilliance of the divine light he encountered was too much for him to bear, ultimately leading him to lose his mind. The Talmud likens his experience to that of a person consuming honey – when taken in moderation, it revives the soul, but in excess, it overwhelms the body, causing one to expel even the small amount that had been beneficial.

The "Other One" (Elisha ben Abuyah) is depicted as someone who, through his deep immersion in occult wisdom, became captivated by the power and authority of the angel Metatron. This led him to the belief that there were, in fact, two gods. When he realized that Metatron possessed the same power as the other angels, he lost his faith entirely. He became a heretic and began to deliberately distort the spiritual insights he had gained in the Orchard. One might say that he could not tolerate the complexity of the Godhead.

Rabbi Akiva is the only one who entered in peace and left in peace, perhaps due to his capacity for simultaneously envisioning the divine in its multiple theophanies *and* the multiplicity of theophanies in the divine unicity that is being theophanized (Subtelny, 2004) – invariance *and* transformations. It seems Rabbi Akiva, much like Bion in Meltzer's description, could sail very far indeed and yet still find his way home in peace, possibly due to his ability for perpetual movement and relatedness between the finite and infinite, between the exoteric and the esoteric, between the sensuous and the non-sensuous.

Hence, approaching O may be a very dangerous task, which may lead to delusion, rivalry with O and megalomania (Bion, 1965). Allowing oneself to be immersed in the emotional experience of the moment is not enough. One has to be able to find one's way safely home. Tragically, the fragile personality gets lost in infinitude and may lose their mind.

As always, Bion seems to be addressing, first and foremost, the analyst's mind. For a truthful apprehension of reality, it is primarily *the analyst* who, with their **analytically trained** intuition, must expand their capacity for surrendering, for temporarily losing themselves in infinitude, remaining open to *anything*, to any logic, that might wander into their orbit, lest they might force their own logic upon the material to which they are exposed. Bion (1965) illustrates this with a patient who says an apparently incomprehensible statement that he knows that his odd job is in the same league as the postman because his friend left white of egg in the bathroom. This may sound insane. However, the relatedness implied by the *patient's* statement sounds incomprehensible since it may be of a different logic than the one to which the *analyst* is accustomed. That is, *the patient's statement may represent phenomena related to each other in an**infinite**universe* in which the relatedness between the phenomena is *beyond* the spectrum of apparent rational logic, or that which is visible to us in a restricted, finite universe. The diameter of the patient's statement may be so vast that one cannot see the opposite side. To approach the patient's different logic, the analyst must renounce *their* logic, or the logic of the conscious, finite, awake mind, and give their imagination an airing – so as to encounter a different logic, irrational, or perhaps "anti-rational", one which, as I mentioned, could be easily dismissed as "insane".

And yet, Bion always reiterates:

> I am not talking about an undisciplined, rhapsodical display of just saying anything that comes into your mind. At the same time, I do not want to be limited by having to be scientific, precise and exact... There *has* to be some sort of disciplinary framework...it *is* somehow necessary so that even your imagination cannot be allowed to develop into an imaginative orgy.
> (Bion 1977c, pp. 51–53)

Going back to the model of the circle, reminiscent of the four who entered the Orchard, one must strive for, albeit never achieve, "an adequate diameter. If it is too small the circular argument becomes a point; if too great it becomes a straight line" (1965, p. 153).

An oneiric state of mind

The point I am trying to stress is that an oneiric state of mind, allowing one to truthfully approach reality beyond the confines of our restricted, human logic, necessitates perpetual movement within a large diameter. Reality, as Bion writes, seems not to obey the laws laid down by the human animal. From this vertex, it is a "reality...no longer distinguishable from dreams, unconsciousness, night... The thinker ha[s] no thoughts, the thoughts [are] without thinkers. Freudian dreams [have] no Freudian free associations; Freudian free associations [have] no dreams..." (Bion, 1975, p. 33).

For that, the analyst must often ignore the deafening noise of the patient's words in order to be able to "hear" what the patient is trying to convey. However, that is very difficult to do. As Bion (1977c) says, we know so much, perhaps too much, about the patient's history, so much about psychoanalysis, medicine, physiology, music, painting and so on, that it is very easy to evade a truthful apprehension of reality, and very difficult to detect this "thing" that we are really observing – or wanting to observe. Moreover, Bion never ceases to remind us of the restrictive and delusive use of words, so often used to reduce the diameter of the circle. He writes, "When I want to indicate something of which I *know* nothing but of which I want to talk or even think, it clothes itself with a meaning and I lose my nothing... My variable becomes a constant" (Bion 1977d, p. 395); the dynamic is rendered static.

Could we then, as Bion suggests, listen to any word as a virtually meaningless term that binds innumerable phenomena which are derivatives of an unknown reality, and then *by letting our minds roam freely*, proceed, indefinitely, to investigate the emotional experience the patient "binds" by that term? We would thus release our grasp on sensuous aspects of reality and embark on a journey that might lead, in Bion's enigmatic, and yet evocative words, "from nothing to unconsciousness to sleep to dream to waking thoughts to dream thoughts to nothingness to O = zero, from O = zero to O which is O = oh! to O which is a picture which is a picture of a hole or greedy mouth or vagina which offers perfect freedom..." (Bion, 1975, p. 36).

"These speculative imaginations, however ridiculous, however neurotic, however psychotic, may nevertheless be stages on the way to what we would ultimately regard as...psycho-analytic formulations" (Bion, 1977e, p. 41).

Since emotional truth is always in transit, in constant flow, it cannot be grasped in a static state, but only in a continuous, dynamic movement which is beyond the capacity of ordinary human consciousness. *Intuition, affording an oneiric state of mind, may thus be the capacity to apprehend* **reality in transience**; not the seemingly static objects that comprise it but *the perpetual movement in and between these objects, allowing for an ever more complex, and therefore more truthful, apprehension of reality* (Bergstein, 2022).

All this dictates a different manner of interpretation too, one that relies less on the content of interpretation and more essentially on facilitating the internalization of a thinking, dreaming object. In this view the analyst's task is to create a setting in which an evolution of a transference process may evolve, be monitored, and be assisted by interpretation. Thus, *interpretation proper* as a meta-psychological statement (with genetic, dynamic, structural, and economic aspects of the transference defined), can be distinguished from more general interpretive *exploration* of the patient's material, which is intended to facilitate its emergence (Meltzer, 1976). An interpretation would thus be a statement *and* a transformation. It not only reveals an existing truth but also provides the means for exploring new connections and wider resonances (cf. Papastergiadis, 2015).

Nonetheless, a so-called psychotic state of mind, in patient or analyst, attempting to avoid pain, is always seeking *to make a dynamic situation static*, re-establishing apparent psychic equilibrium, albeit condemning the person "to live imprisoned in everlasting sanity" (Bion, 1975, p. 35), stifling one's creative capacity. This is the personality's tendency to adopt a "thus far and no further" attitude, a rigidified imprisonment in the past or in the *strived-for* future.

"I know why I dreamed it", a patient says…and I am reminded of Bion's words that

> the patient may be describing a dream, followed by a memory of an incident that occurred on the previous day, followed by an account of some difficulty in his parents' family. The recital may take three or four minutes or longer. The coherence that these facts have in the patient's mind is not relevant to the analyst's problem. His problem…is to ignore that coherence so that he is confronted by the incoherence and experiences incomprehension of what is presented to him. His own analysis should have made it possible for him to tolerate this emotional experience though it involves feelings of doubt and perhaps even persecution. This state must endure, possibly for a short period but probably longer, until a new coherence emerges.
>
> (Bion, 1963, p. 102)

And this too must be a transient meaning that the analyst needs to let go of, so that they can begin a new cycle in pursuit of a new meaning, and so on and on, indefinitely.

Suspending the movement protects the individual from an overwhelming encounter with the emotional turbulence entailed in the ephemeral at-one-ment with O. In fact, it is the *dynamic and inquiring quality* of the interpretation that often evokes evasive reactions, *regardless of its content* (Bion, 1963). This is true of patient and analyst alike. The analyst too can use the interpretation as finite, definite knowledge, as opposed to a provisional, speculative reflection, open to further inquiry, evoking curiosity. Such an interpretation is one in which the "diameter" is too small. Similarly, the interpretation can be too difficult to comprehend, in which the "diameter" is too great. Too small and too large diameters thus indicate defense against emotional turbulence.

The oneiric dimensions of the analyst's mind are often portrayed as those facilitating the uncovering of, or getting in touch with, a patient's deeply buried unconscious experience. However, and this to my mind is the radical notion Bion is introducing into psychoanalysis, the analyst aims not so much at facilitating the transformation of unconscious into conscious, nor is it making the unthinkable thinkable. I suggest it is the infinite *to-and-fro* movement in the doomed-to-fail pursuit of the unknowable that is at the heart of Bion's thinking – restoring the psyche's natural movement between dispersion and cohesion, between intuition and conceptualization, between the finite and the infinite (Bergstein, 2022). The individual can thus become a multi-dimensional personality, that is, a three-dimensional *physical* identity, and a multi-dimensional *psychical* identity (Bion, 1970). It is the very movement that challenges, modifies, stretches and expands our mind endlessly – and is transformative. It is perhaps, as Bion would say, "playing the game for the sake of the game" (Bion, 1982, p. 93).

I would like to end with a story recounted by Yair Garbuz, a renowned painter and writer:

> A man once said to me: "During my trip to Paris, I visited the Orangerie Museum and went down to the hall where Claude Monet's famous panoramic *Water Lilies* is displayed. I looked at it, tried to engage, and made a real effort, but I just couldn't grasp it. From a distance, I could faintly make out the water, with shades of blue, green, and purple, along with lilies and other aquatic plants. I struggled to focus, and I found it difficult to concentrate. I stepped closer, hoping that being near the painting would help me see it better, but instead, the water and lilies vanished. All that remained were thick brushstrokes of paint, layered upon layer. I didn't know what to do… how to look."

"I said to him," Garbuz goes on to write,

> "Respect the wisdom of thy feet. *You* may not have understood it fully, but your body instinctively grasped one of the greatest secrets of *Water Lilies* in particular, and impressionistic painting in general: no matter where you stand, you will always miss something elsewhere. Any conclusion you might form will be shattered as soon as you move closer, or lose its credibility as you move farther away. There is no single correct vantage point from which to observe. The only conclusion we can draw is that we must keep moving, constantly, back and forth, around and around. Only then can we capture as much as possible, and perhaps, something will be revealed. Or not… It is a musical score for the feet…"
> (Garbuz 2014, p. 382).

Notes

1 Meltzer 1980, p. 471.
2 This military metaphor may not only pertain to Bion's war experiences, but is also reminiscent of Freud's description of the analytic encounter as a battle field, a

"struggle between the doctor and the patient, between intellect and instinctual life, between understanding and seeking to act, ... played out almost exclusively in the phenomena of transference" (Freud 1912, p. 108).

References

Bergstein A (2022). "Truth shall spring out of the earth...": The analyst as gatherer of sense impressions. *International Journal of Psychoanalysis* 103:2, 246–263.

Bergstein A (2025). "Buried in the future which has not happened": Non-linear time, non-logic and the ultimate reality of the session. *Modern Psychoanalysis* 49:1.

Bion F (1997). Foreword. In *Taming Wild Thoughts*. London: Karnac, pp. vii–xi.

Bion WR (1963). *Elements of Psychoanalysis*. London: Karnac, 1984.

Bion WR (1964). *Bion's response to Dr Wisdom's review of Learning from Experience*. British Psychoanalytical Society, 17 October 1964 (unpublished).

Bion WR (1965). *Transformations*. London: Karnac, 1984.

Bion WR (1967). Third seminar. In *Wilfred Bion: Los Angeles Seminars and Supervision*, Aguayo J and Malin B (eds.). London: Karnac, 2013, pp. 55–80.

Bion WR (1970). Untitled. In *Cogitations*. London: Karnac, 1992, p. 312.

Bion WR (1975). The dream. In *A Memoir of the Future*. London: Karnac, 1991, pp. 1–217.

Bion WR (1977a). Caesura. In *Two Papers: The Grid and Caesura*. London: Karnac, 1989, pp. 35–56.

Bion WR (1977b). The grid. In *Two Papers: The Grid and Caesura*. London: Karnac, 1989, pp. 1–33.

Bion WR (1977c). New and improved. In *The Complete Works of W.R. Bion*. Vol. 15, Mawson C (ed.). London: Karnac, pp. 45–58.

Bion WR (1977c). *The Tavistock Seminars*. London: Karnac, 2005.

Bion WR (1977d). The past presented. In *A Memoir of the Future*. London: Karnac, 1991, pp. 219–426.

Bion WR (1977e). Untitled. In *Taming Wild Thoughts*. London: Karnac, 1997, pp. 27–51.

Bion WR (1982). *The Long Weekend*. London: Karnac, 2005.

Bion TalamoP (1997). Foreword. In *Taming Wild Thoughts*. London: Karnac, 1997, pp. vii–xi.

Elbaum D (2016). A voice from the flames. In *Makor Rishon*, 5 June (Hebrew).

Freud S (1912). The dynamics of transference. *SE* 12:97–108.

Garbuz Y (2014). *A Home in Galilee*. Tel Aviv: Yedioth Ahronot Books.

Hustwit JR (2007). Process philosophy. *Internet Encyclopedia of Philosophy*. https://iep.utm.edu/processp/.

Meltzer D (1976). Temperature and distance as technical dimensions of interpretation. In *Sincerity and Other Works*, Hahn A (ed.). London: Karnac, 1994, pp. 374–386.

Meltzer D. (1980). The diameter of the circler in Wilfred Bion's work. In *Sincerity and Other Works*, Hahn A (ed.). London: Karnac, 1994, pp. 469–474.

Pascal B (1669). *Pensées and Other Writings*, H Levi (transl.). New York: Oxford University Press, 1999.

Papastergiadis N (2015). John Berger: Between permanent red and the black box of the universe. *South as a State of Mind* 5: 44–49.

Subtelny ME (2004). The tale of the four Sages who entered the Pardes: A Talmudic enigma from a Persian perspective. *Jewish Studies Quarterly* 11: 3–58.
Torres N (2013). Intuition and ultimate reality in psychoanalysis: Bion's implicit use of Bergson and Whitehead's notions. In N Torres and RD Hinshelwood (eds.), *Bion's Sources: The Shaping of His Paradigms*. London and New York: Routledge, pp. 20–34.
Whitehead AN (1925). *Science and the Modern World*. New York: The Free Press.
Whitehead AN (1929). *Process and Reality*. New York: The Free Press.

Chapter 7

A Dream Is Just a Dream

Rudi Vermote

The hypothesis which will be elaborated in this paper is that the oneiric functioning of the mind – of which dreams are a manifestation amongst several other manifestations – corresponds with who we are. It is the stuff that we are made of. We may call it as well 'the mind' or Freud's 'unconscious ego'. In Bion's words it is 'transformation in Knowledge'.

Nevertheless, and hence the title 'a dream is just a dream', although the oneiric function of the mind is an interface with the world and creates ourselves and the world psychically – it is a function that is self-centered, anxiety ridden and it blocks our contact with the infinite, unrepresented field of Being of which we are part. The dynamics between these psychic worlds will be discussed as well as the role of dreaming in them.

This is however not easy, the problem being that words do not really fit to what I hope to transmit.

A model based on Bion's work

Mainly for practical use, I translated Bion's work in zones of psychic functioning (Vermote, 2013, 2020). However it is just a crutch that can be thrown away, a way to help to talk about a wordless reality.

I applied this zonal model to many things like art, love, transference, psychopathology, religion and so forth.

For this lecture, the model of the zones, helps to see the place of oneiric functioning.

The model starts from a statement by Bion:

> the differentiating factor that I wish to introduce is not between conscious and unconscious but between finite and infinite.
>
> (Bion, 1965: 46)

In the model that I present, the differentiating factor is the degree of finite/infinite functioning, not unlike Matte Blanco's (1988) work.

The first zone is Reason

The first zone is Reason or logical verbal thinking. It is fully finite and differentiated.

We are born in a symbolic network with given thoughts and concepts. Education connects us to this web. If not, we are off-grid like some psychotic people.

The zone of verbal thinking is sophisticated and good to solve practical problems. Although sophisticated, it cannot deal with problems with many variables like emotional relationships. Bion called Reason the 'monkey trick business'. It is of not much value for psychoanalytic practice.

You may compare verbal thinking with a GPS: language has no contact with the raw reality but is an ingenious system of reference points just as a GPS has no contact with the road and the wind but is an interface that guides your way very quickly by a satellite system that locates your position on maps.

A downside of the first zone is that reasoning is programmed: we use the same symbols, we are brainwashed so to speak from the beginning of our lives by words and their meaning. As the philosophers Deleuze and Guattari (1987) put it: we live in a shared hallucination and delusion this way.

In the first zone *consciousness, attention and perception* are determined: 'we see what we know' as Goethe said. Reason may order perceptions, thoughts, experiences quickly, but we are blinded by this way of perceiving.

It is also important that in the first zone, *body-mind are separated.*

The second zone

The second zone is a mixed finite/infinite functioning, mixed differentiated and undifferentiated. The second zone corresponds to Freud's dynamic unconscious and M. Klein's phantasies.

It is the zone of thoughts and feelings/emotions. Bion (1963) put thoughts and feelings at the same height in his Grid. Emotions follow the same rules that Freud described for the unconscious: displacement and condensation. Actually – the second zone IS the dynamic unconscious.

The second zone is driven by Freud's pleasure principle, what Bion translated as 'evading pain'. This second zone that we may as well call 'mind' with a small letter m, is also the cradle of anxiety, fear.

The zone is fueled by emotions, senses, perceptions. It makes me think of Bodhidarma's saying: 'the mind is the mind because of things, things are things because of the mind'.

It is the oneiric world not only of dreaming but also of creativity, free association. In this zone representations originate as Bion described it in his books *Elements* (Bion, 1963) and *Transformations* (Bion, 1965).

Bion called mental functioning in this zone: 'dream thought' or 'thinking' or 'reverie' or 'dreamwork alpha'. Note that Bion equalled these concepts.

The oneiric function of our mind goes on night and day: waking dream thought.

In Bion's approach, we are always dreaming, 'I dream therefore I am'. The dream thought is the stuff that we are made of. It is with this function that we are in the world and in contact with ourselves. It is the interface with 'what is' – that we do not know. Therefore it corresponds as well with what Freud described as the unconscious ego.

For use in psychoanalytic practice with psychotic people, Bion made an 'applied psychoanalytic model of thinking', not rational thinking but the associative, spontaneous thinking that takes place in this zone. His model helps us to understand this wonderful device with which we are in the world. We all know this model of Bion's model (Vermote, 2019). Bion operationalized his model in a Grid.

It is peculiar that his model fits well with neuroscientific findings.

Just let me mention a few characteristics of the way Bion looked at 'thinking' or second zone functioning. He saw it as a continuous, automatic, spontaneous, effortless process. Another receptive mind is needed to ignite this thinking in a child. In all his texts Bion stressed *receptivity and passivity* related with this thinking function: we see it in his notions of 'reverie, containment, patience and security'.

You could say that the second zone or mind is a 'pattern generating machine' – detecting effortlessly constant conjunctions in what is unrepresented. It is the spider of T.S. Eliot, the machine in us that creates a web.

This web is a necessary illusion, a veil of illusions, a living protective layer. A kind of coat. In pathologies like psychosis, borderline, psychosomatic diseases, so called actual pathology, this coat has faults.

The second zone tells stories, gives meaning – in contrast with the rational first zone, language in the second zone is a poetic language.

According to Bion, the reverse of the dreaming function is a splitting off – non-thought forming an envious hole, a nameless dread – an evacuation in activities, cutting, drugs.

In the first zone *body and mind* are separated, in the second zone body and mind are less distinct, mind is embodied (for instance: projective identification).

While in the first zone *attention, perception and consciousness* are guided by logical, verbal thought. In the second zone, they are colored by emotions and phantasies. These greatly unconscious phantasies (Klein) or thoughts (Bion) color and determine our perception.

The second zone is the area in which psychoanalysis is working. We deal with it by listening with free floating attention to the freely associating of the patient.

Listening to dreams is privileged phenomenon, not only to see their meaning – but especially to see this second zone at work. These manifest dreams are conscious reflections of the unconscious dream work. In *Cogitations*, Bion (1982) wondered if we even remember night dreams if the dreaming function works well. If the manifest dreams when we wake up are not a kind of overspill. It begs the question. Anyway, our dreams show the functioning of our minds – and how this unconscious functioning integrates, warns, predicts.

The third zone

In his quest for the origin of what is transformed, Bion concluded that we cannot go further than three or four transformations of representations. The Origin of what is transformed falls outside/beyond/behind his Grid of representations in thoughts and feelings.

The Origin is unrepresented, it is fully infinite and undifferentiated. Unknowable and unknown and formless. Bion compared it with Eckhart's Godhead in reference with a represented God. It is the silent unmoved mover.

Bion took an empty symbol to point at it: O.

Furthermore, Bion realized that real psychic change happens at that infinite, undifferentiated, unrepresented, formless level. He stated that only one or two such transformations at that level, in O, are necessary to make an analysis terminable.

This realization was a caesura in Bion's work: he stopped putting 'transformations in Knowledge' of the second zone in abstract formulas and radically went for the experiential and intuitive contact with this world beyond the representations, a world which he called O. A contact that brings a Transformation in O.

Bion found that the language of the mystics is more apt than mathematical functions in trying to put words on a T(O), as the mystics also deal with an unnameable reality that can only be revealed and apprehended-transmitted by experience.

The functioning of the mind beyond the second zone, we may call the third zone or Mind with a capital. This Mind is unrepresented and undifferentiated. At that level of psychic functioning, there is no differentiation between self and other, self and environment: O is becoming O. Mind with a capital is not bound – not carried by space and time.

It is a pure experience going with an absolute perception – knowing without knowing. These words sound meaningless, as they are a cripple trial to word an unnameable experience. Even more: when you can name it, it is not it. As Eckhart said: 'if you can speak about God, it is not God'.

The second zone is the world of desires – drives, pain and pleasure. The third zone does not have these qualities.

Bion (1970) tried to analyze as close to infinity as possible by starving the second zone or mind: 'no senses, no desire, no memory, no understanding, no coherence'.

We need the second zone to let the third zone have an influence on the second zone. It is going to the bottom of the second zone, decreasing its activity at the maximum. This is not unlike the no-mind mind or Mu-shin (Matsuki and Nishihira, 2017). Mind with a capital letter M, the third zone reveals itself with the second zone in an empty state.

In Bion's words, it is then O can get to K, the movement is always from the third zone to the second zone: from O to K, not from K to O.

A kind of nothingness can flow in so to speak. A nothingness that is not nothing, but a kind of full nothingness.

In contact with the third zone, with O, the mind – second zone changes. It becomes less self-centered. The metaphor of the three zones is no longer needed. We are in a no-zone. To paraphrase Keats: at that moment, thoughts and imagination come as natural as a leaf to a tree.

The lifting of the second zone may happen as Bion propagates by a 'no memory, no desire' attitude but may also happen in other ways – like being overwhelmed (the Sublime), transcending in love and sexuality, surprise.

Actually the psychoanalytic method carries some characteristics that may help lifting the second zone: like by not answering as in common communication, listening in free floating attention, silence, receptivity, letting the primary process invade the secondary process of verbal thought, regression to the formless.

In contact with the third zone: a language or action of Achievement (as Bion, 1970, called it – referring to Keats) can take place. The world changes by a word or act that comes from the third zone influencing the second zone, the word is not only a representation any more.

This is the ultimate aim of psychoanalysis:

> What is to be sought is an activity that is both the restoration of god (The Mother) and the evolution of god (the formless, infinite, ineffable, non-existent) which can be found only in the state in which there is NO memory, desire, understanding (Bion, 1970, p. 129)

Clinical example

The patient is a man with a self-defeating behavior for many years – manifesting itself in an extreme procrastination.

My reasoning or Zone 1 thinking about him brought ideas of oedipal rivalry – which was manifest in his phantasies and some of his relationships. Also some narcissistic problems and envy could explain his situation. This kind of first zone approach was however not so helpful. Moreover I did not feel any rivalry in the transference – countertransference.

I was mainly struck by a discrepancy between his talents and his sportive and handsome attitude and his deep lack of interest in anything.

In the sessions, the analysand freely associated but without much emotion.

One day he told me a history of what sounded like a childhood trauma; he needed surgery as a child; and the hospital staff had not allowed his parents to be present in the hospital, at least this is the way that he remembered it. This memory was as well brought in an emotionless way. Was it a kind of screen memory?

He had a romantic relationship since years but suffered from anhedonia without other signs of depression.

I decided to be in an empty state of mind as much as possible.

One day we had suddenly a shared feeling as if looking in a deep hole in the floor. Freezingly looking in the depth. It felt like a kind of becoming – sharing and intuition.

At this moment he told me a deeper childhood trauma and now in a very vivid tone – when he was two years old – his parents had found him stifled by the terror of a tyrannic-sadistic nanny who had later been dismissed.

In a flash it became clear that he had refrained from life, as a defense. Blocking spontaneous and playful behavior.

The following session the word 'goesting' (in Dutch) popped up in my mind. It is a stronger word than appetite or desire – and applies to eating, sex and feeling vital. In Dutch it is a kind of embodied word. It did not emerge in a chain of associations, it popped up in relation to this shared experience.

We may call it a kind of 'language of achievement' – a word that not only communicates but also does something.

The word touched the patient and brought a change.

References

Bion, W.R. (1963/1984). *Elements of Psychoanalysis*, London: Karnac.
Bion, W.R. (1965/1984). *Transformations*, London: Karnac.
Bion, W.R. (1970/1986). *Attention and Interpretation*, London: Karnac.
Bion, W.R. (1982/1992). *Cogitations*, London: Karnac.
Deleuze, G. and Guattari, F. (1987). *A Thousand Plateaus*. Trans. B. Massumi. Minneapolis: University of Minneapolis.
Matte Blanco, I. (1988). *Thinking, Feeling and Being: Clinical Reflections on the Fundamental Antinomy of Human Beings*. London: Routledge.
Nishihira, T. and Matsuki, K. (2017). *"Mu-shin no Taiwa" (Dialogue of Mind-No Mind)*. Osaka: Sogensha.
Vermote, R. (2013). The Undifferentiated Zone of Psychic Functioning: An Integrative Approach and Clinical Implications, *Bulletin of the European Federation of Psychoanalysis*, 13, 16–27.
Vermote, R. (2019). *Reading Bion: A Chronological Exploration of Bion's Writings*. In D. Birksted-Breen. The New Library of Psychoanalysis Teaching Series. London: Routledge.
Vermote, R. (2020). Psychic functioning outside of mental representations. Implications for psychoanalysis, *The Journal of the Japan Psychoanalytic Society*, 20, 2: 3–16.

Chapter 8

The Oneiric Dimensions of the Mind in the Analytic Session[1]

João Carlos Braga[2]

The theme *the Oneiric Dimensions of the Mind* offers us the opportunity to examine one of the most significant inflections in clinical psychoanalytic thinking over the last decades. Bion's contributions in *Transformations* (Bion, 1965) introduced a paradigm shift that has changed analytic work in many ways. One of these changes is our understanding of the oneiric dimensions. The traditional view of the oneiric dimension as the stage for the development of representations (dream-work in Freud, dream work in Bion) has been replaced by a view of this dimension encompassing several mental *spaces* with different mediums and processes, a cradle for proto-thoughts and emotions, where what is infinite is transformed in finite and undifferentiated psychic elements develop into differentiated forms of mental products.

From a conceptual perspective, this change moves the focus of the analyst from *contained* to the processes and mediums of *containment*, or from the differentiated to the undifferentiated zone of the personality (Vermote, 2011, 2019), or, yet, from representations to transformations (Sandler, 2005). Four different mental spaces with their own mediums and processes are at stake: knowledge, minus knowledge, hallucinosis, and being or becoming at one with the object (Bion, 1965).

In an attempt to contribute to the study of this novel proposition, I will explore these different oneiric dimensions by presenting and discussing a clinical session using different levels of abstraction. My option of focusing and expanding on the clinical experience, instead of moving to a theoretical discussion, is an epistemological choice that I share with many colleagues from São Paulo's Brazilian Psychoanalytical Society. This choice is rooted in the thought that, from *Transformations* onwards, Bion progressively privileged the psychoanalytic work with the unknown, having emotions as the analytic compass and intuition as the analyst's main implement.

The oneiric dimensions of the mind in the analytical room

Stan arrives at the session visibly tense. He was about to undergo a prostate biopsy for a suspicious image that was detected by ultrasound, a finding that

DOI: 10.4324/9781003482512-9

he had talked about during previous sessions. He talks in detail about the biopsy and his ideas about it. He extends his observations to memories surrounding his father's death due to the same disease which, even before undergoing the biopsy, Stan already believed that he had. He highlights the fact that his current age is the same as his father's when he died.

While listening to him, I feel increasingly uncomfortable. That session would be the last one before my summer vacation, and I start to consider postponing my trip to avoid leaving him alone at that difficult moment. These feelings and thoughts make me aware of the presence of guilt.

The emotional atmosphere in the session is intense and has hints of terror. Suddenly, Stan mentions bluntly: *I thought I wouldn't tell you, but I've already decided that if the biopsy shows cancer, I won't come back for the sessions.* His surprising comment makes me more uncomfortable and is followed by his silence as if he were waiting for my response. After a tense moment, I say to him: *We don't know what the biopsy will show, but we can both already follow that you are having doubts about our condition of dealing together with a situation that is very scary for you.* My words seem to wake him up to my presence and he begins to include me in his associations. He points out two or three situations in which he recognizes the analysis as playing an important role in his life and surprises me by describing a dream, which he rarely did in his sessions. In his dream, he arrives at one of his sessions, and the door to the consultation room is closed. While in the waiting room, he somehow knew that I was in session with a boy and, because of that, I was not going to call him in. He also realizes in the dream that there was a party going on in another part of the house, to which he was not invited. After describing this dream, he makes no associations but adds casually that the boy was 9 years old.

After describing the dream, Stan remains silent. His description makes me feel deeply disturbed and perplexed because, the next day, I was traveling on vacation to meet with family members and celebrate my 9-year-old grandson's birthday, which had been strongly present in my mind. I make a brief assessment of the situation, but I am unable to identify possible sources from where Stan could have known this information about my personal life. I feel compelled to intervene but, at the same time, unsure about what path to take. My first thought was to follow the path of symbolic formation and propose the idea of him being the boy – and not the adult – who primarily needed my care. However, my emotional experience weighs on me, and after some hesitation and struggle with my fears, I tell him: *It seems to me that you have a knowledge not known to you, the knowledge that there is a boy with whom I am going to be with when I leave you at this very difficult time for you.* A heavy, prolonged silence follows as if both of us had lost the grounds on which we stood. Stan looks very surprised by my unusual statement, and I am amazed at the experience that I am living. The atmosphere in the session becomes awkward, disturbing, and overwhelming, but the tension eases gradually. As the session continues, a layer of deep intimacy emerges between us. His communications begin to flow easily, opening possibilities for us to look at the ongoing emotional situation from various vertices. Stan communicates his belief that he was facing an imminent disaster and revives, with lively emotion, memories of situations that had already been analyzed. He brings up rivalries that he had with his younger sister since childhood, delusional beliefs about a predetermined fate of a cancer death following his family history, and the fact that he had to be resigned to subordinate positions in affective relationships based on his certainty that his father had always preferred his sister instead of him. He appeared to be self-analyzing in my presence, and my participation for the remaining of the session becomes limited to punctual interventions and expansions (approximations and integrations) of his elaborations. As an example, I point out to him that what he was doing in my company was like revising a poorly elaborated draft.

A few complementary observations about the session

My communication to Stan (*a boy with whom I am going to be when I leave you*) was not mentioned again in the session or during the continuation of his analytical work. In my evaluation, this communication served as a catalyst in a chemical reaction, in which it stimulates but does not participate as a reagent. Had I opted for an analytic intervention based on the contents of the dream (as symbolic, transferential, or projective identifications), the analytic work would be directed to the dimension of knowledge – and not to the realization that there was something being lived at that moment in the session, albeit unknown and even unknowable. I accepted to enter a terrain that, for me, was not only unknown but also treated as forbidden in the analytical work (the reference to an element belonging to the analyst's personal life).

This episode appeared to be a turning point in the session, furthering a more integrated analytic contact. My intervention seemed to help bring together different layers of Stan's mental functioning. Strong anxieties stimulated by the imminent separation in the analytic work evolved as unelaborated emotional experiences resurfacing as conscious memories, fantasies of abandonment and helplessness, and, possibly, primordial terror and guilt. From the oneiric perspective, my intervention favored the creation of a space for dream-work (*dreams, quasi-dreams,* and *non-dreams,* as discriminated by Rezze, 2001) experienced with terror and barely supported in his mind, emerging from an unknown background.

Later, I felt convinced that what I had lived with Stan was a very important experience for both of us, in which something from my mind, in a mysterious way, became available to him. My observation about my personal experience, validating his oneiric capture, seemed to have had the effect of revealing an exceptional emotional convergence between us, an experience of being *at one* that expanded his mental space as well as mine.

An inclusive look at the session: A row C approach

In my evaluation, at the beginning of the session, Stan was strongly trying to get rid of painful ideas and feelings, ignoring the present experience that he was living with me. The discharge of intolerable emotional experiences revealed the work of a hallucinatory layer of his psychic functioning. He had no doubts about the reality of his ideas.

After my intervention pointed out his disbelief in the capacity of the analysis to deal with his terror, a second movement occurred in the session, in which his frame of mind changed. I evaluate this as a move toward accepting the contact with the analytic situation, including my existence as a possible container for his painful emotional experiences, scattered infantile memories, hallucinosis, information, and delusions – a movement triggered by the incoming prostate biopsy and my vacation. The oneiric dimension at that moment follows the pattern of the knowledge dimension (thoughts of the thinker). This second movement culminates with Stan's surprising description of something that he named *a dream*, which strongly suggests evidence of a fragment of my psyche being processed by him.

Let us consider that after my intervention (*...you have a knowledge not known to you...*), another change occurred in Stan's frame of mind in the session, now encompassing elements of *being* or *becoming*. My intervention seems to have uncovered the fact that the analytical situation was including an experience of analyst and analysand *being at one*, in the way of "becoming real" (Bion, 1970, p. 32).

Following this experience, a fourth movement emerged in the session, *i.e.*, Stan's endurance of a state of mind marked by a lively presence that allows a psychoanalytic conversation. We can identify this movement as the mutative development of emotional intimacy and convergence, well described by Eshel 2019, p. 1) as the stages of *presencing, withnessing*, and *two-in-oneness*.

Reading the oneiric dimensions of the mind in the session at a conceptual level

This session illustrates distinct processes of transformations occurring in different oneiric mediums on the way from undifferentiated to differentiated conditions in the psyche. Clinical observations allow the identification of distinct groups of transformations occurring in different mental spaces: thoughts (knowledge), "without-ness"[3] (minus knowledge), false thoughts (hallucinosis), and experiences of *being at one with*.

Emotions can be seen as vectors conducting undifferentiated elements, as proposed by Bion: *The emotions fulfil a similar function for the psyche to that of the senses in relation to objects in space and time* (Bion, 1961, p. 119). In the session, we can conjecture the presence of emotions in the very primordial stage: primitive anxieties of separation (evoked by the analyst's vacation) and annihilation (fantasies about death in the identification with his father), plus unthinkable terror and guilt.

The raw materials of these transformations are fragmented mental registers of prior experiences with internal and external reality, especially non-elaborated oedipal fragments, stimulated by the experience of Stan being part of the analytic pair. These elements fill a-sensuous empty patterns (Vermote, 2016) similar to basic assumptions in groups, providing the stage for the processing of a kind of "psychic mill."

Observed from this perspective, oneiric dimensions are battlefields where the fate of undifferentiated elements is decided and worked through by distinct processes of transformations. This condition would be comparable to the development of stem cells which, depending on various factors, can develop into different specialized cells, more mature in form and function than the original cells.

Evidently, the interventions of the analyst interfere with the development of oneiric processes in the analysand; they can either stimulate or inhibit elements of different processes that create one of the following outsets:

- New thoughts, such as reveries and oneiric images pictured directly or through derivative narratives (Ferro, 1993 2003; Rocha Barros, 2000)
- Without-ness, the stripping of meanings, intolerance to the kind or intensities of specific emotions (minus knowledge)
- Hallucinosis, the reverse of alpha function, to occupy the *space* of potential real thoughts
- A sustained condition of *being at one with the other*, favoring an analytic conversation

Further ideas on the oneiric dimensions of the mind

The section above was a conceptual approach written from a knowledge perspective (Row F in the Grid). If we look closer at the clinical experience, we can also observe it from the perspective of the Grid's Row C, *i.e.*, imaginative, and rational conjectures as personal myths (Bion, 1963, p. 12; 1970, p. 18).

The view from this perspective is fundamental in establishing the condition of the conjectures as products of a single mind, *i.e.*, based on the analyst's impressions of the experience. This is the utmost (finite) psychoanalytical possibility when we look from the perspective of O, the unknown, *the void and formless infinite*. It highlights the analyst's choice of trying to operate psychoanalytically with elements from the undifferentiated zone of mental functioning (Vermote, 2011, 2019) of both participants. Putting it differently, the final form of transformations in the various oneiric dimensions of the mind (*signifiers*). Thoughts (knowledge), blanks where knowledge could be present (minus knowledge), imagination taken as facts (hallucinosis), and analyst and analysand being at one compose the oneiric dimensions of the mind explored in psychoanalysis to date.

Wrapping up: Are we glimpsing at another oneiric dimension of the mind, beyond being at one with the object?

The approach to the oneiric dimensions favors enchantment but raises difficult questions. The analysand's "dream", in the session described above, brings attention to one particular point: can we claim psychoanalytical evidence that somehow experiences of one mind (in this case, the analyst's) are caught and dreamt by another mind (the analysand's) without sensorial communication? Could we be glimpsing yet another oneiric dimension of the mind?

In *The Italian Seminars*, Bion (1977) elaborates on a question by one of the analysts participating in the seminar. The analyst describes his clinical experience with an analysand, who reported a dream with events very similar to the ones that the analyst had painfully lived just hours before. Bion answers cautiously but positively about the possible existence in humans of other senses beyond the common ones that we recognize and the sixth sense that he (Bion, 1970, p. 7) had conceptualized as intuition. He mentions:

> *But the questions that have been raised here may mean that we have to become aware of the possibility that there are other receptor organs of which we are not aware.*
> (Bion, 1977, p. 64)

This same conjecture of the possible existence of "other senses", primordial ones, can also be found a few pages before the above quote, where Bion recalls four clinical experiences of which he mentions:

> *… to draw the patients' attention to vestiges of acute observation – so acute that they could not stand the information that their primordial senses brought them.*
> (Bion, 1977, p. 52)

What we are speculating here is that the development of a deep interconnection between analyst and analysand (*being at one with O*) moves the boundaries to the unknown. With the prior boundaries (intuition and at-one-ment) conquered and now being a common ground for many analysts, new phenomena call for a psychoanalytical investigation. In this endeavor, *the oneiric dimensions of the mind* continue to offer us facets where we can catch glimpses of the passion lived by Freud, Klein, Bion, and many other psychoanalysts that preceded us. Now, it is our turn to investigate this new horizon.

Notes

1 Bion International Conference – Mexico, November 10–13, 2022.
2 São Paulo's Brazilian Psychoanalytic Society; Curitiba's Psychoanalytic Group, Brazil.
3 Notation proposed by Sandler (2005, p. 381).

References

Bion, W. R. (1961). A theory of thinking. *Int. J. Psychoan.*, 43, Parts 4–5, 306–310.
Bion, W. R. (1963). *Elements of Psycho-analysis*. London, William Heinemann, 1963.
Bion, W. R. (1965). *Transformations*. London, Karnac, 1991.
Bion, W. R. (1970). *Attention and Interpretation*. London, Karnac, 1993.
Bion, W. R. (1975 [1977]). Caesura. In: *Two Papers: The Grid and Caesura*. Rio de Janeiro, Imago Ed., 1977.
Bion, W. R. (1977). *The Italian Seminars*. London, Karnac, 2005.
Eshel, O. (2019). *The Emergence of Analytic Oneness – Into the Heart of Psychoanalysis*. London, Routledge.
Ferro, A. (1993). From Hallucination to Dream: From Evacuation to the Tolerability of Pain in the Analysis of a Preadolescent. *Psychoanal. Review*, 80 (3), 389–404.
Ferro, A. (1999). O Sonho da Vigilia: Teoria e Clínica. *Rev. Bras. Psican.*, 33 (3), 449–458. [The Awakened Dream: Theory and Clinic.]
Ferro, A. (2003). O Pensamento Clínico de Antonino Ferro. Conferências e Seminários. França, M.O.F. and Petricciani, M. (Org.). São Paulo, Casa do Psicólogo, 2009. [*Antonino Ferro's Clinical Thinking – Conferences and Seminars.*]
Levine, H. (2016). Myth, Dream and Meaning: Reflections on a Comment by Bion. In: *The W.R. Bion Tradition*. Levine, H., and Civitarese, G. (Eds.). London, Karnac.
Rezze, C. J. (2001) – O Sonho, o Quase Sonho e o Não Sonho. In: Bion<>SBPSP – Seminários Paulistas. França, M.O.F., Thomé, M.C.I., Petricciani, M. (Org.). São Paulo, Casa do Psicólogo, 2001. [The Dream, Quasi-Dream and Non-Dream. In: *Bion<->SBPSP – Sao Paulo's Seminars.*]
Rocha Barros, E.M. (2000) – O processo de constituição de significado na vida mental: afeto e imagem pictográfica. *Rev. Bras. Psicanal.*, 34 (1), 111–121. [Affect and Pictographic Image: The Constitution of Meaning in Mental Life]
Sandler, P.C. (2005). *The Language of Bion – A Dictionary of Concepts*. London, Karnac.
Vermote, R. (2011). On the Value of 'Late Bion' to Analytic Theory and Practice. *Int. J. Psycho-Analysis*, 92: 1089–1098.
Vermote, R. (2016). Era Bion um kleiniano?Conferência na SBPSP, 28-10-2016. [*Was Bion a Kleinian?*Conference at Brazilian Psychoanalytic Society of São Paulo, 10-28-2016.]
Vermote, R. (2019). *Reading Bion*. London, Routledge.

Chapter 9

Learning from Experience in the Analytic Session
Dream-Work-Alfa

Antonio Sapienza

---

dream-work-alfa; psychotic ↔ non-psychotic personality; primordial mind; barrier of contact

Introduction

In essence, this paper is addressed to analysts with clinical experience. It highlights the basic qualities of the analytical equipment that allow us to "dream" the ongoing session in the analysis room.

In the introduction of *The Interpretation of Dreams*, Freud (1900) states the subjective meaning of this magistral text: his reaction to his father's death, which he considers the most poignant loss in a man's life. In its initial pages, through an excerpt from Virgil's *Aeneid* (book VII), "*Flectere si nequeo superos, Acheronta movebo*",[1] Freud emphasizes his proposal, by overpassing turbulences, to search and rescue the mental desires rejected by the higher mental agencies, those repressed dream-desires that disturb the underworld (Unconscious) and "require" listening.

I will first examine from the psychoanalytic vertex four groups of factors in the analyst's personality related to the methodological equipment that provides basic support in clinical practice for the discrimination, interaction, and correlation between internal and external reality, in view of learning from emotional experience with the analysand.

Next, in the second part of the paper, I reintroduce the mythical model of the "Death Pit of the Royal Cemetery of Ur", initially presented by Bion in "The Grid" (1977) and resumed by the same author in his "First Conference in São Paulo" (1973). Two visual images are highlighted as constructs:[2] 1. The Burial Ceremony at the Royal Death Pit of Ur; and 2. The Royal Tomb Plundering.

The four groups of factors in the analyst's personality

1. At each session, the analyst must experience mental pain while being able to maintain the fluidity of unconscious waking thought.

The physician considers recognition of pain subordinate to its cure; the psychoanalyst's view is expressed by Doctor Samuel Johnson's letter dated September 21, 1758, to Benet Langton (as found in James Boswell's *Life of Samuel Johnson*):

> *whether to see life as it is, will give us much consolation, I know not; but the consolation which is drawn from truth, if any there be, is solid and durable; that which may be derived from error must be, like its original, fallacious and fugitive.*
>
> (Bion, 1970, ch. 2)

The analyst's ideal state of mind in the analytic session must allow for substantial contact with mental pain within the oscillating experiences of the paranoid-schizoid and depressive positions (PS ⊠ D), the partnership's daily journey that will require the exercise of the analyst's virtues of patience, perseverance, and security in maintaining the fluidity for unconscious waking thinking.

The support of these mental conditions of the analyst has a strong connection with the maximum liberation from scotomas and psychopathological obstructions (hence, the utmost importance of his personal analysis). This specific analyst's inner freedom will depend on the cultivation of his own mental discipline and the methodological experience of "opacification" of memories, theories, and desires, aiming at the expansion of containment and receptivity to the communications of the analysand's unconscious phantasies and ideas. The analyst's floating attention will accompany the analysand's free associations.

The ability of tolerating mental pain, without evading it, is essentially related to the conditions of preservation and viability of the matrices of primitive thought, that is, unconscious phantasies and preconceptions containing emotional violence, potentially capable of becoming "civilized" when freed from omnipotence. The qualitative and quantitative contents of the matrices of primitive thought are protected by the contact-barrier, the state of which will depend on the greater or lesser fluidity and readiness of the unconscious intuition, as well as the degree of precision and adequacy of the analyst's capacity of observation in face of the ongoing emotional experience with the analysand.

Therein lies the guarantee of the two-way path: conscious ⊠ unconscious (double-track mind), which will allow the adequate correlation between dream-thought (C), preconception (D), and conceptual thought (F), without interpretative hastiness, mental saturation, or psychosomatic blocks of the analyst.

2. The elaboration of dream-work-alfa (Bion, 1992) will be accomplished by the analyst, operating psychic changes able to generate emotional learning

intimately linked to the experience of the ongoing session in the bi-personal interaction field.

> *Indeed, consciousness of an external reality depends on the person's ability to tolerate being reminded of an internal reality. Relationship between the external and internal reality is thus similar to the relationship between preconception and the realization approximating to it. It is reminiscent of Plato's theory of Forms.*
>
> (Bion 1965, 86)

The value of the analyst's reverie function (Bion, 1967),[3], [4] implied in Bion's above quoted proposition that is supported and nourished from the reserves of certain mental elements, the alpha elements, is directly involved in dream-work-alfa (Bion, 1992, 62), with which the learning from emotional experience and the expansion of life and psychic reality becomes possible. Without the sufficiency of the concurrent alpha elements, threats of mental impoverishment and psychic death begin to predominate: concretism, omnipotence, omniscience, fanaticism, rigidity, and mental narrowing, with greedy dependence on the sensory world and its more frequent phenomenology: hallucinosis, acting-out life, mental misery, stupor, and megalomania.

We must keep in mind the dual function of the contact-barrier in the modulation between Conscious and Unconscious (Bion, 1962):

1. To protect the Unconscious from the excesses of stimuli coming from external reality which could lead to the damage of the matrices of unconscious phantasies as well as to their buffering and sealing, resulting in a robotization phenomenology.
2. To regulate the speed and non-massive character of the projective identifications of the unconscious world towards external reality, thus preventing the invasive flow and the flooding effects of the Unconscious in external Reality, with the consequent phenomena of confusion, delusional experiences, strangeness, and depersonalization crises.

The analyst's verbal language will be a direct expression of the contact barrier state of his psychic apparatus in contact with his analysand.

3. The analyst needs to know how to sustain, promote, and develop equipment for "dreams-thoughts".

> Perhaps it may seem to you that our theories are a kind of mythology and, in the present case, one that is unpleasant. But in the end, is not every science a kind of mythology like this? Can't the same be said today of your own physics?
>
> (Freud, 1933, p. 211)

I think that the emphasis that Bion gives to psychoanalytic research, privileging the K link in the search for the unknown, for the infinite (K ↔ O), favors the use of psychoanalysis, as a scientific deductive system, unconstrained from rigidity and dogmatism. At the same time, it favors the exercise of psychoanalytic practice with freshness and vitality, as a live method of probing the most primitive strata of human mental life.

The instrumental flexibility of psychoanalysis, in other words, its *non-ossification* without false eclecticism, can be expanded since analysts respect the strong interdependence between mythical thinking (C Category) and its evolution into scientific thinking (F, G, H Categories). Schematically: C ↔ F, G, H.

At this point, I would like to resume Karl R. Popper's (1982) statement: Science advances in order to verify ideas, images of the world. Science comes from myth. This can be seen very clearly in the primitive scientists, namely in the primitive Greek philosophers, in the pre-Socratic philosophers who were still very influenced by the formation of the myths. The questions they pose are, however, entirely rational. By rational questions, I mean questions oriented towards the truth.

It is interesting to consider the interrelations between "myth, dreams, and unconscious thought" to the point that Bion placed them in the same C category of the genetic axis of the Grid (Bion, 1963).

The following functions of unconscious waking thought are highlighted in *Cogitations* (Bion, 1992, 181):

a   the ability to elaborate and use dream-thoughts (Category C of the Grid).
b   the memory capacity (notation).
c   the use of all the functions of the psychic apparatus, which Freud suggests will come into existence with the dominance of the Reality Principle.[5]

4. The analyst will have to "dream" the analytic session: his well-trained intuitive capacity will be his mainstay.

> The dream-memory is the memory of psychic reality and constitutes the heart of the analysis.
>
> (Bion, 1970, 70)

The analyst must remain awake and perform the function of "dreaming" the session; therefore, his sleeping needs must be satisfied. The emanation of analogies or "as if" thoughts on his mental screen, will provide the analyst with a substrate for the evolving of the emotional experience since these dream-memories will be possibly used with discernment in his verbal formulations.

It is expected that the analyst's analysis has allowed him to realize a considerable part of his "personal myths", with an emphasis on the positive and negative aspects of the Oedipus Complex. Therefore, it should be noted that the alpha function will be at the service of the "myths'" fabrication, now in his experience with his analysand, and that these "dreams" should be defined and communicable, still having some commonsense qualities as well as non-common sense (Bion, 1992, 186).

One could locate the alpha function in a kind of living frontier which seems to be the place where the thought is formed, like a mountain crest, which seems to be the cradle of the cloud's formation (Bion, 1944, 7–21).

Exercises in rereading the analytic experience outside the analytic session, in the light of mythical elements,[6] are useful for reparation and invigoration of the analyst's intuition (Bion, 1992, 240). The analyst's "dreaming" in tune with the alpha function guarantees the floating attention, the counterpart of the patient's free associations, supporting Transformations towards the "O" of the ongoing session.

Thus, for example, the near destruction of the language of achievement in a session or period of sessions may be correlated to attacks and punishments of a jealous deity, attentive to establishing and developing the confusion of languages among people interested in building a new city. The same model, the Tower of Babel, can be useful in understanding the endless controversies and struggles between the representatives of the so-called psychoanalytic "schools". The concept itself is considered metaphorically by Bion as "a cavity or a pit where the thought is buried" (1977, 44).

Death Pit of the Royal Cemetery of Ur: First Scene: Burial Ceremony (3500 B.C.); Second Scene: Plundering (3000 B.C.)

> Unless psychoanalysis develops a technique analogous to that archaeology, we shall not know what was in the hearts and minds of those courtiers of Ur, Abraham's City, when they walked into that death pit, took their potion and died.
>
> (Bion, 1977, 8)

Thinking about the importance of illustrating a psychoanalytic exercise that aims to provide and favor the storage of alpha elements, in the form of unconscious visual thoughts, dreams, and myths (Bion, 1992, 238), I decided to reintroduce the two scenes highlighted by Bion in his description of the "Death Pit of the Royal Cemetery of Ur", adding some elements of personal reading and reflection. I invite the reader to consider the four groups of psychoanalytic factors already exposed.

I think that a reflexive and critical reading of this model proposed by Bion may have highly salubrious effects for us, the analysts, sharpening further the importance in clinical practice of the microscopic observation of the four groups of factors examined in the first part of this paper.

This narrative is chosen for its vivid pictorial qualities (C category on the grid) as well as for its suitability in psychoanalytic practice to serve as a construct, in view of the specificities of the analytic work dealing with the catastrophic layers which often underlie psychotic suffering. It shares dream-thoughts qualities with the well-known myths of Oedipus, the Garden of Eden, the Tower of Babel, and the Death of Palinurus (Virgil's *Aeneid*, Book VI). Bion referred to them as a cast of panels making up a mythical gallery available for the analyst's reverie functions.

In 1927 and 1928, Sir Charles Leonard Woolley (1880–1960), aged 47, was engaged in excavations in the city of Ur, the legendary homeland of Patriarch Abraham, the current city of Al-Muqayyar, Iraq. For about twelve years, he dedicated himself to the discovery of royal pits in the sacred area of the Cemetery of Ur, whose beginnings date back to 3500 B.C. Among more than a thousand tombs from this early period, only sixteen were royal tombs. Joint expeditions by the British Museum and the University of Pennsylvania Museum continued this work.

Bion tells us the story of the Royal Cemetery of Ur as a kind of fable, making use of the time gap of about five hundred years between the burial ceremony and the plundering. He highlights two scenes rich in pictorial images: the first corresponds to the burial of the king (year 3500 B.C.) and the second relates to the looting of the royal tomb (year 3000 B.C.).

First visual image: "The Burial Ceremony in the Death Pit of the Royal Cemetery of Ur" (3500 B.C.)

On the death of the king, a large well was dug and accessed by an inclined ramp, the Death Pit. In the well, a tomb was built, and the body of the dead king was carried into it, surrounded by offerings, as well as two or three of his closest servants, killed to continue to serve the sovereign.

The ceremony included a procession formed by all the nobles of the monarch's court dressing in their finest clothes and decked out in their finest jewels. They processed towards the bottom of the well with musical accompaniment and dances.

In this religious ritual, each noble poured himself a small goblet containing narcotics, possibly hashish; then they lay down, falling asleep. From above, the priests and acolytes poured the earth taken from the well over them, burying the sleeping ones and the burial chamber. Next, the earth was trodden underfoot, becoming a new floor, thus preparing the place for a future ceremony. Thereby, the filling of the well was done through a relatively slow process, in stages (Woolley, 1966, 234).

It is assumed that Magic managed to sanctify the chosen place, the City's rubbish dump, covering up the royal spoils and thus masking the view that human spoils were nothing but filth. Paradoxically, the place's sacralization attracted those who were looking for a place to rest their own dead "filth" in an environment coated with magical properties. As time went by, the hallowed place lost its sacred character on account of other burials, becoming vulgarized.

Second visual image: "The Plundering of the Royal Tomb" (3000 B.C.)

A very different procession took place at the same site without any publicity about five hundred years later: the tombs began to be plundered in the third dynasty.

Royal grave robbers dared to face fears linked to "spirits of Death" and the ghostly "sentinels of the dead" installed by the powers of the Religion of Ur. Therefore, they managed to steal the treasures hidden in a place guarded by evil and threatening spirits.

The tomb raiders may be regarded as the forerunners of Science for their courage and curiosity for profiting during their adventure in a domain mostly left under the guard of taboos of Magic, Religion, and Death.

Bion proposes this reconstruction as an archaeological transformation of the expeditions initiated by Sir Leonard Woolley. From his point of view, it allows us to delineate a wide emotional territory which psychoanalysts must deal with in romantically primitive terms and a state of condensation: constructs.

In "The Future of an Illusion", Freud (1927) considers belief in God an illusion but, at the same time, he has no doubt about the reality of illusion: "beliefs" and "illusions" must be taken seriously by psychoanalysts. Against this background, Bion thinks that the interpretation of omnipotence is particularly unfortunate for it opposes construction, besides reducing the constant conjunction helplessness-omnipotence to the single term omnipotence.

Final Considerations

Returning to the Myth of the "Death Pit", a few questions can be considered:

1 What is the price paid to enter the ceremonial space of Ur? How powerful must the emotional, cultural, and religious force be, to the point of being able to impose on a group of people a well-defined course of action leading the grieving nobles to their death, without apparent opposition? (On November 18, 1978, in Guyana, about 900 followers of Reverend Jim Jones, leader of the People's Temple, died in a ritual mass suicide: another demonstration of the power of Religion, Ritual, Magic, and Drugs.)
2 If a child, and psychoanalysis is still in its infancy, does something so dangerous as to lose his life, is it correct to say that it is ignorance? Or is it more appropriate to assert the existence of dynamic impulses that led to his death?

3 Should we be attentive in considering our "religious" hierarchy sufficiently awakened to the risks of becoming spiritual descendants of the Ur priests' Religion?
4 The royal burial group seemingly had taken, one by one, a narcotic drug before being buried alive: hashish. Wasn't some force more powerful than the drug itself at work in their minds, even before the monarch's death, sealing their hearts in a deadly pact?
5 What would be the drug used by the looters of the royal tomb? The curiosity? The courage and the thirst for profit? It opposes the hostility and omnipotence of which deity?
6 What is the health prospect required to challenge those murderous forces to overcome the terrors that inhabited the "Death Pit"?
7 How did the thieves come to penetrate the earth through tunnels and passages so narrow with such precision, also finding the Queen's tomb? Was it luck?
8 Should we build monuments to the plunders of the Royal Tomb as pioneers of Science, as scientific as our scientists? Or should we consider a good part of today's scientists as deservers of insults for their greed and resigned conformism?
9 Insofar as the psychoanalyst's "act of faith" is the search for the development of more experience and knowledge in each session, will this "Religion: Love for the Truth" be enough to prevent psychoanalysis from becoming a new "opium of the people"?
10 Wouldn't the ideal of "a definitive and safe cure" be for psychoanalysts also a suicidal pact or, at least, an invitation to early retirement, that is, the condition of becoming "buried alive"?

I think that the "price of freedom is and must continue to be eternal vigilance", in order to preserve the struggle for the vitality of psychoanalysis against the risks of its ritualistic reification, besides the analytic pair daring to enter dead ends.[7]

I finish this exposition by borrowing the opening of the fifth chapter of Pour une Esthétique Psychanaiytique, "Escher ou la fascination du sans fonde", where Murielle Gagnebin (1994) proposes the following:

Passionate about pushing back the limits of figurability as far as possible, artists find psychoanalysts concerned with accompanying their patients to the frontiers of the analyzable. But, in this effort for more representation, lucidity, here and there, finds an opposing force that seems to grow in the same rhythm as the expression, as if the accurate ideal of figuration engendered an adverse principle. Intimately committed to the delicate problem of exposing a saying always elusive, Aesthetics and Psychoanalysis seem like this, each in their way, placed in defiance in face of the unrepresentable.

(p. 36)

In their Introduction to the Italian edition of *Trasmissione della Vita Psichica tra Generazioni* (Kaer et al., 1995), Antonino Ferro and Anna Meregnani consider that:

> *(...) a work authentically psychoanalytic is accompanied by the ability to broaden the field it investigates. Metapsychologically, it does not become a cage that opposes the new.*

Notes

1 "If I cannot bend the Olympus gods, I will turn over the Acheron."
2 Construct: it is an arbitrary and fictitious schema, not inferred from experience as the hypothesis is. Even if it does not constitute a true picture of the actual state of affairs, it satisfies the human imagination and prompts further investigations (e.g., atoms in Physics) (Runes, 1969).
3 The analyst's reverie function: it has characteristics of empathic and detoxicating reception similar to the "maternal gaze"; it allows the patient to "mirror himself" in the analyst, in a relational area, leaving in the shadow all sympathetically "humanistic" ambition; it allows the analyst to present to his analysand what he believes he "sees", without fear; through compassion and truth, it offers resources to repair the damages of the patient's thinking (unthinkable anguish) in the experiences of nameless terror.
4 "Rêverie": a) On a visit to Nemours in 1844, Victor Hugo went out at dusk to see some bizarre sandstone. Night comes, the city is silent, where is the city? "All this was not a city, not a church, not a name, not color, not light, not shadow: it was reverie. I remained motionless for a long time, gently allowing myself to be penetrated by this inexpressible ensemble, by the serenity of the sky, by the melancholy of the hour. I don't know what was going on in my spirit and I couldn't say it, it was one of those ineffable moments, when one feels in one's own being something that falls asleep and something that awakens". b) In "The Man Who Laughs", Victor Hugo writes: "The observed sea is a reverie" (Bachelard, 1993).
5 See the main psychic functions treated by Freud: sense perception, consciousness, memory, attention, inquiry, action, and thought.
6 Myth: Fantastic narration of gods and heroes, which belongs to the cultural heritage of a people. Founded on an oral or written tradition, it usually has a close link with religion, forming the reason for beliefs, taboos, and rites. It often constitutes a support (base) to the social system and an explanatory key to natural phenomena (Edigeo, 1992, 1178).
7 In a personal communication, Darcy Antonio Portolese (SBPSP) comments the following: "The issue of tolerating mental pain, without evading it, seems to me to be the basic matrix from which meaning may arise, or the introjection of an object that tolerates the meaninglessness".

References

Bachelard, G. 1993. *La Poétique de la Reverie*. Paris: P.U.F.
Bion, T.P. 1944. Las Estructuras Mentales Escondidas [The hidden mental structures]. *Rev. Psicoanalisis AP de BA* 16 (1): 7–21.

Bion, W.R. 1962. *Learning from Experience*. London: Heinemann.
Bion, W.R. 1963. *Elements of Psychoanalysis*. London: Heinemann.
Bion, W.R. 1965. *Transformations*. London: Heinemann.
Bion, W.R. 1967. *Second Thoughts*. London: Heinemann.
Bion, W.R. 1970. *Attention and Interpretation*. London: Tavistock Ltd.
Bion, W.R. 1973. *Bion's Brazilian Lectures - 1 São Paulo*. Rio de Janeiro: Imago.
Bion, W.R. 1977. *Two Papers: 'The Grid' and 'Caesura'*. Rio de Janeiro: Imago.
Bion, W.R. 1992. *Cogitations*. London: Karnac.
Edigeo. 1992. *Enciclopedia Zanichelli. Dizionario enciclopedico di arti, scienze, tecniche, lettere, filosofia, storia, geografia, diritto, economia*. Bologna: Zanichelli.
Freud, S. 1900. *The Interpretation of Dreams S.E.*, Vol. IV. London: Hogarth Press.
Freud, S. 1911. *Formulations on Two Principles of Mental Functioning. S.E.*, Vol. XII. London: Hogarth Press.
Freud, S. 1927. *The Future of an Illusion. S. E.*, Vol. XXI. London: Hogarth Press.
Freud, S. 1933 [1932]. *Why War? S.E.*, Vol. XXII. London: Hogarth Press.
Gagnebin, M. 1994. *Pour une Esthétique Psychanaiytique*. Paris: P.U.F. https://www.puf.com/content/Pour_une_esth%C3%A9tique_psychanalytique.
Kaer, R., H. Faimberg, M. Enriquez, and J.J. Baranes. 1995. *Trasmissione della Vita Psichica Tra Generazioni*. Roma: Ed. Borla.
Popper, K. 1982. Offene Gesellschaft - offenes Universum. Franz Kreuzer im Gespräch. *Sociedade Aberta, Universo Aberto*. Lisboa: Publicações Dom Quixote.
Runes, D. (ed.) 1969. *Dictionary of Philosophy*. Barcelona: Ed. Grijalbo.
Woolley, C.L. 1966. "Os Túmulos Reais de Ur". [The royal graves of Ur.] In *O Mundo da Arqueologia* [*The world of archaeology: The pioneers tell their own story*], edited by C.W. Ceram, 233–237. São Paulo: Cia. Melhoramentos.

Chapter 10

Cézanne Dreams Bion

Robert Snell

In August 1978, the year before he died, Bion noted a patient's dream of being swept away down a river towards a weir. 'I tell you, I never woke up so fast in my life', said the patient. Bion asks himself what, 'according to me, was he talking about?' Was the patient in danger of becoming, 'like me', too wide-awake, 'too conscious, too rational'? Or too fast asleep – 'in fact, the sleep of death'? Was he in the state of mind of 'the sleep of psychoanalysis'? Bion goes on to quote Milton: 'There plant eyes, all mist from thence purge and disperse, that I might see and tell of things invisible to mortal sight' (*Paradise Lost*, Book 3).

But, he continues:

> "telling of things invisible to mortal sight" ... cannot ... be bought by "losing" mortal sight; to be blind, unconscious, unaware of the world visible and audible ... is not the solution. One must dare to be aware – consciously – of the universe that is apparent in the state of mind in which one is asleep *and* the state of mind appropriate to "awake", Yin and Yang... Therefore merely being able to concourse musically, balletically, athletically, is not enough; it must be an intercourse – a means of communication "inter", between two states of mind. Socrates described himself as a mental midwife; perhaps the psycho-analyst is a midwife between two states of mind of the analysand: for example, Maths + Art of Fugue, Cézanne + La Montagne Sainte-Victoire.
>
> (Bion, 1994, pp. 366–367)

I want to focus on this 'Cézanne' state of mind, which was capable of giving birth to La Montagne Sainte-Victoire.[1] Cézanne, I think, dared confront Bion's questions in the context of his own art, and the painter might shed light ('*dar luz*') on the psychoanalyst. We shall I hope find ourselves in Row C of the Grid (myth, dream, culture) – for since Bion, it is hard to believe that any cultural development, including his own great innovations, could be born unless previously dreamed: b to a, sensation to picture.

DOI: 10.4324/9781003482512-11

And Paul Cézanne (1839–1906) was not just one cultural precedent among many. Known as the 'the father of modern art', like Bion he was responsible for a major paradigm shift: away from de-coding and interpreting towards the creation, in his field, of a means of perceiving/thinking, of *making representable*. 'At the core of the Cézannian revolution', wrote the painter's biographer Alex Danchev, 'is a decisive shift in the emphasis of observation, from the description of the thing apprehended to the process of apprehension itself' (Danchev 2013, p. 338).

'Cézanne', in inverted commas, might almost be a voice – combative, gnarled, insistent, humble, under few illusions – from *A Memoir of the Future*. 'This blasted métier ... brings all your theories to grief', he said (Gasquet 1921 and 1926, p. 147). 'Old as I am, I'm only just starting out' (Borély 1902, p. 19). The elderly Bion could be a little more upbeat. 'At 75, I think I am beginning to get the hang of it' (Vermote 2019, p. 5).

Bion was himself a landscape painter. 'What sort of artist are you?' he asked his audience of analysts in Paris in 1978; 'a great many analysts don't really know what sort of artists they are'. 'So although your tendency may be to say you don't paint, I say you do. Therefore, get out your colours' (Bion 1978).

Antonino Ferro and Giuseppe Civitarese, who have done more than anyone to elaborate upon the aesthetic dimension of Bionian and post-Bionian psychoanalysis, sum up thus:

> we are artists, Bion suggests, or, at least we should have the courage to use our skills as artists – after all, don't we all dream at night and during the day? Don't we all compose the poetry of the mind that Freud (1891) talks about in his book *On Aphasia*? Don't we all constantly transform sensory reality into images, sounds, colours, all possible kinds of pictograms, audiograms etc. olfactograms, and then assemble these fragments into narratives, paintings, olfactory melodies, musical odours, and so on.
> (Ferro and Civitarese 2015, pp. 30–31)

This is the operation of what Bion termed a-function, a transformation of elements that are unknowable in themselves, b-elements, primitive sensations, 'affective, pre-categorical and semiotic' (Civitarese 2018, pp. 5–6), into something else, a-elements and combinations of a-elements, to create something new in itself and as yet unknown, a transformation whose paradigm is the dream.[2]

It is a dimension of human creativity perhaps more explicitly touched upon by Cézanne than by any other painter in the history of art. He liked to refer to what he called his 'sensations', or his 'petite sensation': 'those confused sensations that we bring with us into the world' (letter to Joachim Gasquet, 3 June 1899, in Cézanne 2013). 'To paint', said Cézanne, 'is to record one's coloured sensations' (Denis 1907, pp. 177–178). Like Bion, Cézanne did not make such gnomic statements idly.

Cézanne's 'sensations' might allow us glimpses of the process of alphabetisation in action, the next best thing perhaps to some psychic CERN accelerator yet to be invented. Perhaps the 'sensation' was an intimation of b-elements – elements from the painter's proto-mental, semiotic world – stirring through his sense impressions, through contact with sensual experiences from the outside, from 'nature' (which must of course always imply 'human nature' too). In other words, the first hint of an a-element in formation, a caesura-moment. The 'sensation' to which Cézanne referred is already a contact barrier.

Rudi Vermote reminds us that in French the word 'sensation' corresponds more closely to a physical experience, while in English, as Didier Anzieu observed, it involves something psychic: 'an idea as sensation ... which is still vivid and sensorial but already appropriated by the psyche', like Proust's madeleine – which would be an example of an a-element (Vermote 2019, p. 103). For all Bion's suspicion of the evidence of the senses, of which we are 'prisoners' (Bion 1978a, p. 21), his thinking always draws us back to the earliest embodied sensations, the ultimate source of thinking itself.

So how did Cézanne, and how might we, stay open to these primordial and profoundly generative 'sensations'?

Here is some supervision from Cézanne, in conversation with a younger friend, Joachim Gasquet:

CÉZANNE: ... if one day I interpret more than I should, if today I am carried away by a theory which opposes that of the day before, if I think as I paint, if I intervene ... bang! All's lost! [*patatras! Tout fout le camp!*]
GASQUET: What do you mean, intervene?
CÉZANNE: The artist is only a receiver of sensations, a brain, a registering apparatus [*un réceptacle de sensations, un cerveau, un appareil enregistreur*] ... A good apparatus of course, fragile and complex, especially in relation to others ... But if he intervenes, if, paltry as he is, he dares deliberately to interfere with what he must translate, then his own mediocrity filters through. The work produced is inferior.(Gasquet 1921 and 1926, p. 109).

He must therefore proceed 'without memory and desire' (Bion 1967). 'Cézanne stood before nature with a commitment to forget everything' ['*avec le parti pris de tout oublier*'], wrote the painter Emile Bernard (Bernard 1904, p. 33).

Cézanne's metaphor of a 'registering apparatus' for his 'sensations' strikingly echoes Freud's 'telephone receiver' of very few years later (Freud, 1912, pp. 114–115), receptive to messages from the unconscious. 'Vision' does not seem essential for this apparatus: indeed Freud recommended the analyst voluntarily blinding himself, and Bion (nevertheless reverting to a visual metaphor) suggested the need for 'a penetrating beam of darkness: a reciprocal of the searchlight' (Bion 1990, pp. 20–21; Grotstein 2007 [2018]).

At the same time, as Bion insisted in 1978, '"telling of things invisible to mortal sight" cannot … be bought by "losing" mortal sight'; one must also dare to be awake.

Indeed perhaps *need* to be awake, for there was risk involved, the risk a river swimmer runs of being swept into a weir.[3] Cézanne was highly alert to this: the danger of being pulled under, into a confusion (Denis 1907, p. 94) of unalphabetised primordial sensations, or perhaps of 'balpha' elements, into the matrix of b-elements that is also the source of vitality and without which no transformation can happen. 'Sensation' was not always pleasant, and the painter was, to the last, wide-awake to the threat of chaos. One of his favourite works of literature was Balzac's novella *Le chef-d'oeuvre inconnu*, about a fictional painter named Frenhofer who produced a vast, ambitious, but ultimately chaotic and unreadable painting. 'Frenhofer, c'est moi', Cézanne told Emile Bernard, jabbing at his chest (Snell 2021, pp. 123–126).

The difficult task, as the Sibyl warns Aeneas, is not to descend into Hades but 'to retrace your steps, to find the way back to daylight' (Virgil 1962, Book VI, lines 128–9, pp. 122–123). A lifelong love of Virgil is something else Cézanne shared with Bion.

There is the necessity of finding a viewpoint, a vertex, if the miracle of transformation is to happen, rather than the catastrophe of overwhelm in the underworld.

'Here on the riverbank the motifs multiply', Cézanne wrote to his son in 1906, 'the same subject seen from a different angle offers subject for study of the most powerful interest and so varied that I think I could occupy myself for months without changing place, leaning now more to the right, now more to the left' (letter of 8 September 1906, Cézanne 2013, pp. 370–371).

It is not *just* a question of keeping relatively still, so that 'sensation' might do its work and 'selected facts' might emerge from multiplicity. As Cézanne and Merleau-Ponty remind us (e.g. Merleau-Ponty 1964, pp. 58–59), the artist/observer/analyst is mobile, in the landscape, part of the field, too. The smallest shift in position changes the view, and this fact of our embodied existence must also be taken into account in the search for representation and must be considered not as an obstacle but as integral to the experience whose fullness is being sought. To insist on a static, monocular vision is perhaps 'a sleep of death', from which the patient, and the viewer of the painting, really should be awoken.

So how in practice is the artist/analyst to proceed? The mature Cézanne's answer would be: touch by coloured touch: the pigment on the artist's brush / the live, emotionally coloured, maybe minimal intervention or response by the analyst. Therefore, says Bion, 'get out your colours! … Use a few simple colours like blue, black, yellow, green …' (Bion 1978). I think he is talking about what Ferro and his colleagues from Pavia call 'unsaturated' interpretations.

Here is Cézanne speaking with Joachim Gasquet as he works the portrait of Joachim's father, his old friend Henri Gasquet:

> [E]ach brushstroke I make is a little of my blood mixed with a little of your father's blood, in the sunshine, in the light, in the colour, and … there is a mysterious exchange that goes from his soul which he knows nothing about to my eye which recreates it, and in which he'll recognise himself … each touch must correspond, there on my canvas, to a breath of the world, to the light over there on his whiskers, on his cheek. We must live in accord, my model, my colour and I, together shading in the same passing minute. If you think it's easy painting a portrait.
>
> (Gasquet 1921 and 1926, pp. 151–154)

Cézanne's coloured 'touches' on the canvas must be living, 'correspond to a breath of the world'. They are both deliberated and spontaneous, assured and experimental, ways in which he seeks to attune himself and his canvas to his subject and his experience of being with his subject, in time and space. In one respect they are the brushstrokes of Impressionism, attempts to find finely calibrated equivalents to the optical sensations generated by the *motif*. But they are also far more embodied than this. They mediate not just between the experience of his eyes and the canvas, but between the canvas and the 'sensations' to which Cézanne gave such particular and hard-to-define meaning, his overall psychosomatic, mental/emotional 'sense' of his subject, in relation to him. A little later in his life, he spoke of *'sensations colorantes'*, sensations that *give* colour and light (Bernard 1907, p. 78). In this respect the coloured touches might be thought about as 'dreamed' responses in action, forms of reverie, both wakeful and dreamy. Each, furthermore, interacts with the coloured marks already in place, requiring a new response, and in the process, in this instance of a portrait, the subject might come to recognise himself.[4]

Painting by means of coloured touches is thus a form of dreaming with open eyes, or perhaps with eyes both shut and open, of 'waking dream thought'. Alphabetisation is set in train, each touch a building block towards thought and representation. If, as the painter Sargy Mann wrote, there is 'nothing to distract … from the patient attention to colour', it will 'in time build an experience … utterly real and utterly unknown' (Mann, 1996).

Bion wrote in *Transformations*:

> The psycho-analyst's domain is that which lies between the point where a man receives sense impressions and the point where he gives expression to the transformation that has taken place. The principles of this investigation must be the same whether the medium is painting music, mathematics, sculpture, or a relationship between two people, whether expressed verbally or by any other means.
>
> (Bion 1965 [1984], p. 46)

If the principles are the same, perhaps the painter can help us flesh out the process. Indeed, if 'sensation' is active as well as passive, Cézanne is showing us something of what must animate that critical domain between reception and expression.

For both painter and analyst, all this is in the service of +K, of linkage, and of building an ever more flexible and accommodating 'container'.

'Look at this,' said Cézanne, holding his hands apart, fingers spread wide, bringing them very slowly together, then squeezing and contracting them until they were interlocked.

> That's what one needs to achieve. If one hand is too high, or too low, the whole thing is ruined. There mustn't be a single slack link, a single gap through which the emotion, the light, the truth can escape. I advance all of my canvas at the same time ... I approach all the scattered pieces ... Everything we look at disperses and vanishes, doesn't it? Nature is always the same, and yet nothing of what appears to us remains. It is our art's job to convey the thrill of nature's permanence [*le frisson de sa durée*] along with the elements and the appearance of all its changes. We must taste her as eternal. What is behind her? Maybe nothing. Perhaps everything. Everything, do you understand? So I join together her straying hands ... I take from right and left, here, there, everywhere, tones, colours, shades, I set them down, I bring them together ... They make lines. They become objects, rocks, trees, without me thinking about it ... They take on volume. They have a value. If these volumes, these values correspond in my sensibility and on my canvas to the planes, the marks that I have there and are in front of our eyes, well, my canvas joins hands. It doesn't waver. It goes neither too high nor too low. It is true, it has density, it is full.
> (Gasquet, 1921 and 1926, pp. 108–109, and see Gasquet, 1991, p. 148)

From Negative Capability, to attunement through 'selected facts', to the creation of a secure 'container', to transformation in 'O': this is the order of experience towards which Gasquet's Cézanne seems to be pointing us. The transformation that occurs when, in Bion's words, 'perceptions of the patient's material' cohere 'to form his representation of O' is analogous 'to that of the painter who transforms the landscape into a painting' (Bion 1965 [1984], p. 25). The psychoanalyst who succeeds in a 'steady exclusion of memory and desire ... will have the consolation of building his psychoanalytic technique on a firm basis of intuiting evolution'. Just as for Cézanne in front of his canvas, the 'evolving session is unmistakeable and the intuiting of it does not deteriorate' (Bion 1967, p. 19).

This container-building process is also the creation of a transformative 'dream space'. A parallel reality starts to manifest itself, in the session as on the blank screen of the canvas, something both utterly real and utterly unknown. It is a transformation and transfiguration of the concrete. It is what the poet Rilke discerned when, in 1907, he was standing in front of Cézanne's *Madame Cézanne in a Red Armchair*. The chair, he wrote, seemed 'so perfectly translated into its painterly equivalents that, while it is fully achieved and given as an object, its bourgeois reality at the same time relinquishes all its heaviness to a final and definitive picture-existence' (Rilke 2002, pp. 71–72).

It is akin to what Ferro touched upon when he wrote about metabolising a patient's 'boulder of pain', transforming it into something that can be dreamed and shared (Ferro and Nicoli 2017, pp. 137–138). The massive mountain's 'picture existence' is what allows it so incontrovertibly to be what it is, La Montagne Sainte-Victoire; simultaneously, it is relieved of its heaviness. The final picture is the record of an evolution of here-and-now experiences; and, like a session, it *is* a here-and-now experience in itself, which, if we can stay with it, is healing because it can put us in touch with our own wider dimensionalities, our capacity for simultaneity, to be or think more than one thing at a time, as in a nocturnal dream. In these senses art can be spoken of as an expansion of the 'container', personal and cultural – and this of course, for Bion, Ferro and post-Bionians, is the aim of therapy. In psychoanalysis, for Bion, we are dealing with quintessentially aesthetic transformation.

Bion's emphasis on 'binocular vision' was central to his teaching: the ability to 'oscillate', change vertices or points of view and hold them in tension, and in this way to allow an 'intercourse between two states of mind', above all between waking and sleeping. It is not just a question of inventiveness or skill ('musical … athletic … balletic'). Proceeding by coloured 'touches' seems inevitably and inexorably to lead to a greater and greater breakdown and fragmentation of 'surface' sense and logic, to an increased tension between Yin and Yang, logicalities and illogicalities, and a greater porosity in the membrane separating waking from sleep. In this way what emerges on the canvas, in the session, in the patient, in the analyst, in the field, takes on both the 'variety' Bion spoke of – of 'moods, ideas and attitudes' (Bion 1967, p. 18) – and Cézanne's 'volume … value', fullness. And more.

Cézanne's art, to quote Rudi Vermote writing about Bion's 'contact barrier', is a 'living semi-permeable membrane composed of alpha elements', and this, while it separates conscious and unconscious, also preserves, with a degree of tension that varies from painting to painting, a sense of the intimacy of the relations between conscious and unconscious (Vermote 2019, p. 16). I think it is because of this tension and this intimacy that Cézanne's work can be so extraordinarily compelling.

'Essence and existence, imaginary and real, visible and invisible – painting scrambles all our categories, spreading out before us its oneiric universe of carnal essences, convincing resemblances, mute significations', wrote Merleau-Ponty (1964, p. 35, my translation). In the dissolving forms of the late, great 'Mont Sainte-Victoire' in Basle, the colour distances itself from the motif to take on a life of its own, but, in an extreme tension, is somehow still the mountain. In the Philadelphia 'Bathers' we see strange cyphers of bodies that nevertheless invite visceral, somatic responses, 'neither flesh nor fleshless', to invoke T. S. Eliot (1936, p. 191). And a similar 'mixing and blurring of categories', like that which Edna O'Shaughnessy deplored in *A Memoir of the Future* (O'Shaughnessy 2005, pp. 1523–1524), is evident in the passage from *Cogitations* quoted at the start. What *is* the nature of the pairing the 'Maths' state of mind in relation to 'Art of Fugue', and the 'Cézanne' state of mind in relation to 'La Montagne Sainte-Victoire'? Perhaps it has some bearing on the question of authorship, or location in the Grid? But the answer, as Bion was fond of quoting Blanchot, might be the misfortune of the question (Blanchot 1969 [1992], p. 15). In the process of transcending the caesura, painter and analyst are midwives for a constant, surprising, often unsettling, sometimes painful, often joyous birthing – 'at the cutting edge of aliveness' (Grotstein 2000, p. 691).

When Cézanne wrote to his son from the riverbank, it was right at the end of his life, during the stiflingly hot summer of 1906. He had escaped from his work on the Philadelphia 'Bathers' to the banks of the river Arc, where he and Zola and their friends had bathed as boys. Perhaps, suggests Alex Danchev, Cézanne often found himself thinking of Virgil in that place – perhaps of Book VI of *The Aeneid*, and the shade of his father. Aeneas found his father not far from a crowd of ghosts along the banks of the Lethe, souls waiting for reincarnation. These ghosts, if they are to return to earth and dwell in flesh and blood, must, in Virgil's words, be *'immemores'*, with memory washed out (Virgil 1962, Book VI, line 750, p. 141; Danchev 2013, pp. 352–353). Might we also sense an identification on the painter's part with these dead – blind, without memory, familiar with the underworld and its secrets – but who are also about to be reborn? Perhaps the river Arc also evoked the mythical underground river Alpheus in *The Aeneid* Book III, which only surfaces now and then, 'a secret passage … beneath the sea-bed' (Virgil 1962, Book III, lines 695–6, p. 68), the sacred river 'Alph' of Coleridge's dream-poem *Kubla Khan*. Bion compared 'waking dream thought' with this mythical river: 'a continuous process belonging to the waking life and in action all through the waking hours, but not usually observable' (Bion 1994, p. 38; Vermote 2019, pp. 82–83). Alph-Alpha: the Arc/Alph as Cézanne's final 'frontier of dreaming' (Ogden 2002), in which 'flesh and blood' meet psyche, soul.

Notes

1 This and other paintings referred to in the text can be found in Snell 2021.
2 '"[B]eta elements," those primitive pre-thoughts or non-recognized proto-affects that await a mind to think them by "alpha-bet(a)-izing" them via alpha function

into alpha elements that can then enter into "mental digestion" as memories, feelings, and thoughts' (Grotstein 2000, p. 690).
3 *Sublime Subjects* (Civitarese 2018, pp. 77–82).
4 True reverie is by definition unwelcome, said Antonino Ferro. It is insistent, grating, and takes you over (Ferro and Niccoli 2017, pp. 70–72). Flaubert, Cézanne reminded Gasquet, saw the colour purple when he was writing his novel *Salammbô*. When Cézanne himself was painting his 'Old Woman with a Rosary', he saw 'un ton Flaubert', 'something indefinable, a blueish, russet colour that, it seems to me, comes off *Madame Bovary*. It was no good reading Apuleius, which I did to try to get rid of this obsession, because for a time I thought it was dangerous, too literary. Nothing would do it. That great blue russet colour had got a hold on me, sang in my soul. My whole being was bathed in it' (Gasquet 1921 and 1926, p. 111).

References

Bernard, E. (1904). Paul Cézanne (*L'Occident*, July 1904), in Doran, P. M. (ed.) (1978). *Conversations avec Cézanne. Emile Bernard, Maurice Denis, Joachim Gasquet, Gustave Geffroy, Karl-Ernst Osthaus, R. P. Rivière, et J. F. Schnerb, Ambroise Vollard, etc*. Paris: Macula.
Bernard, E. (1907). Souvenirs sur Paul Cézanne (*Mercure de France*), in Doran, P. M. (ed.) (1978). *Conversations avec Cézanne. Emile Bernard, Maurice Denis, Joachim Gasquet, Gustave Geffroy, Karl-Ernst Osthaus, R. P. Rivière, et J. F. Schnerb, Ambroise Vollard, etc*. Paris: Macula.
Bion, W. R. (1965 [1984]). *Transformations*. London: Karnac.
Bion, W. R. (1967). Notes on memory and desire. In Spillius, E. B. (ed.) (1988). *Melanie Klein Today. Developments in Theory and Practice*. Volume 2: Mainly Practice. London and New York: Routledge, 17–21.
Bion, W. R. (1967 [1984]). *Second Thoughts. Selected Papers on Psycho-Analysis*. London: Karnac.
Bion, W. R. (1978a). *Four Discussions with W. R. Bion*. Perthshire: Clunie Press.
Bion, W. R. (1978 [2019]). A Paris Seminar. In *The Complete Works of W. R. Bion*. Edited by C. Mawson and F. Bion. London: Routledge.
Bion, W. R. (1990) *Brazilian Lectures: 1973 São Paulo; 1974 Rio de Janeiro/São Paulo*. London: Karnac.
Bion, W. R. (1994). *Cogitations*. New Extended Edition. Edited by F. Bion. London: Karnac.
Blanchot, M. (1969 [1992]). *The Infinite Conversation*. Translation and Foreword by S. Hanson. Minneapolis and London: University of Minnesota Press.
Borély, J. (1902). Cézanne à Aix. In Doran, P. M. (ed.) (1978). *Conversations avec Cézanne. Emile Bernard, Maurice Denis, Joachim Gasquet, Gustave Geffroy, Karl-Ernst Osthaus, R. P. Rivière, et J. F. Schnerb, Ambroise Vollard, etc*. Paris: Macula.
Cézanne, P. (2013). *The Letters of Paul Cézanne*. Edited and translated by A. Danchev. London: Thames and Hudson.
Civitarese, G. (2018). *Sublime Subjects. Aesthetic Experience and Intersubjectivity in Psychoanalysis*. London and New York: Routledge.
Danchev, A. (2013). *Cézanne. A Life*. London: Profile Books.

Denis, M. (1907). *Cézanne*. In Doran, P. M. (ed.) (1978). *Conversations avec Cézanne. Emile Bernard, Maurice Denis, Joachim Gasquet, Gustave Geffroy, Karl-Ernst Osthaus, R. P. Rivière, et J. F. Schnerb, Ambroise Vollard, etc.* Paris: Macula.

Doran, P. M. (ed.) (1978). *Conversations avec Cézanne. Emile Bernard, Maurice Denis, Joachim Gasquet, Gustave Geffroy, Karl-Ernst Osthaus, R. P. Rivière, et J. F. Schnerb, Ambroise Vollard, etc.* Paris: Macula.

Eliot, T. S. (1936). *Burnt Norton, from Four Quartets*. In *Collected Poems 1909–1962*. London and Boston: Faber and Faber, 1974.

Ferro, A. and Civitarese, G. (2015). *The Analytic Field and its Transformations*. London: Karnac.

Ferro, A. and Nicoli, L. (2017). *The New Analyst's Guide to the Galaxy. Questions about Contemporary Psychoanalysis*. London and New York: Routledge.

Freud, S. (1912). Recommendations to Physicians Practising Psycho-analysis. *The Standard Edition of the Complete Psychological Works of Sigmund Freud*, Volume XII (1911–1913): The Case of Schreber, Papers on Technique and Other Works, 109–120. London: Hogarth Press.

Gasquet, J. (1921 and 1926). Cézanne. Conflation of three dialogues from the two editions in which they first appeared. In Doran, P. M. (ed.) (1978). *Conversations avec Cézanne. Emile Bernard, Maurice Denis, Joachim Gasquet, Gustave Geffroy, Karl-Ernst Osthaus, R. P. Rivière, et J. F. Schnerb, Ambroise Vollard, etc.* Paris: Macula.

Gasquet, J. (1991). *Joachim Gasquet's Cézanne. A Memoir with Conversations*. Translated by C. Pemberton, Preface by J. Rewald, Introduction by R. Schiff. London: Thames and Hudson.

Grotstein, J. S. (2000). Notes on Bion's 'Memory and Desire'. *Journal of the American Academy of Psychoanalysis*, 28 (4): 687–694.

Grotstein, J. S. (2007 [2018]). *A Beam of Intense Darkness. Wilfred Bion's Legacy to Psychoanalysis*. London: Routledge.

Laplanche, J. (1992). *Seduction, Translation, Drives*. London: Institute of Contemporary Arts.

Mann, S. (1996). Shared Experience: Selected by Semir Zeki for the Philosophical Transactions of The Royal Society. *Sargy Mann Archive*. http://sargymannarchive.com/sargy-mann-writings/shared-experience/. First consulted 29.04.19.

Merleau-Ponty, M. (1964). *L'œil et l'esprit*. Paris: Gallimard, 1983.

Ogden, T. H. (2002) *Conversations at the Frontier of Dreaming*. London: Karnac.

O'Shaughnessy, E. (2005). Whose Bion?*Int. J. Psycho-Anal.* (8)86, 1523–1528.

Rilke, R. M. (2002). *Letters on Cézanne*. Translated by J. Agee. New York: North Point Press.

Snell, R. (2021). *Cézanne and the Post-Bionian Field: An Exploration and a Meditation*. London and New York: Routledge.

Spillius, E. B. (ed.) (1988). *Melanie Klein Today. Developments in Theory and Practice*. Volume 2: Mainly Practice. London and New York: Routledge.

Vermote, R. (2019). *Reading Bion*. London and New York: Routledge.

Virgil (1962) *The Aeneid*. Translated by C. Day Lewis. London: The New English Library.

Chapter 11

Oneiric Dimensions of the Mind in Frida Kahlo

Jani Santamaría Linares

Before I describe my experience of dreaming the oneiric dimensions of Frida Kahlo, two sets of introductory comments are required: the first addresses the relation between artistic models and psychoanalysis and, the second addresses metaphors of the artistic field in the consulting room.

Bion began his *Transformations* (1965) using artistic models. In it, he exemplifies how a painter manifests "his poppy field" on a canvas, which may not be identical to the original.

> For Ferro and his colleagues, the traditional relationship between art and psychoanalysis needs rethinking. "Psychoanalysis should not be used, as it so often is, to decipher an artistic text, but ... instead art should serve to interpret psychoanalysis ... [in] a meeting, a collaboration or an opening" (Ferro & Civitarese 2015, p. 63). They have a parallel function, and the former can illuminate the latter. Art's opening would seem to lead to the oscillating poles of pleasure – the pleasure of narrating and representing – and of tragedy (...).
>
> (Snell, 2023, p. 129)

Thus, art is not seen as a pleasurable entertainment providing escape from frustration. On the contrary, it appears as a growth-promoting activity whose aim is to enable the unknown to be grasped and to achieve mental growth.

> [W]e are artists, Bion suggests, or, at least we should have the courage to use our skills as artists—after all, don't we all dream at night and during the day? Don't we all compose the poetry of the mind that Freud ([1891] 1953) talks about in his book *On Aphasia*? Don't we all constantly transform sensory reality into images, sounds, colours, all possible kinds of pictograms, audiograms etc., olfactograms, and then assemble these fragments into narratives, paintings, olfactory melodies, musical odours, and so on (Civitarese & Ferro, 2015, pp. 30–31).
>
> (Snell, 2023, p. 127)

DOI: 10.4324/9781003482512-12

Bion borrows analogies from the artistic field when he discusses concerns about the problem of communication among psychoanalysts and above all communication between the analyst and the patient. He wrote:

> listening to the conversation between yourself and your patient, what language is being talked, either by him or her, or yourself, or both of you? Don't write notes about this story, make some marks on paper. Use a few simple colours like blue, black, yellow, green. Then look at it; there you will get an idea of how that patient struck you. If you were a musician, what kind of music would you compose? If you were a writer, what language would you choose?
>
> (Bion, 2014a [1978], p. 203)

He added: "you will have to be able to have a chance of feeling that the interpretation you give is a beautiful one, or that you get a beautiful response from the patient. This aesthetic element of beauty makes a very difficult situation tolerable" (2014a, p. 211).

For instance, in the consulting room, Ferro writes:

> I become aware of the qualities of my verbal painting, of the shading of tones, of certain characteristics of my colours, and I "learn to paint" from the patient who teaches me to make paintings which correspond increasingly to what she feels and experiences in the session.
>
> (Ferro, 1999, p. 48)[1]

Bion was himself a landscape painter; he insisted on the metaphor of artistic creation in all of his work. For him, the analyst must be like a painter; as a painter, we must know how to use our palette of colors, emotions, and dreams. So, said Bion: "Get out your colors!" "What sort of artist are you?", he asked his audience of analysts in Paris in 1978; "a great many analysts do not know what sort of artists they are". "So although your tendency may be to say you do not paint, I say you do. Therefore, get out your colors" (Bion, 2014a [1978]).

The color I choose to start my chapter is a comment that Bion mentioned in an interview with a Mexican colleague who visited him in Los Angeles in 1978, intending to invite him to visit our country. He said, "If we take the case of Mexico, it seems to me that we would find a great culture with an enormous historical background" (Bion, 2014a [1978], p. 218).

Who better than Bion to describe the landscape in which the Mexican painter Frida Kahlo grew up?

As Mycroft, a character in *A Memoir of the Future*, writes,

> The amount of material is sometimes so abundant that it is doubtful that a psychoanalyst can "interpret" the model with the efficacy of a computer. Thus, what is needed now is a procedure or an instrument capable of

revealing the configurations. (Let us use intuition and common sense.) (Bion, 1991, p. 99)

Feeling authorized by Mycroft to use my intuition and common sense and knowing how complex it is to talk about Frida Kahlo,[2] a Mexican legend, I asked myself, where should I approach this iconic artist? I let the question float momentarily and asked in reverse: How should I NOT approach a presentation on Frida Kahlo? I guess that Bion answered my question precisely in the interview I mentioned in 1978, as follows:

> If we saw a group of Mexicans together, would we have any way of knowing that they were from Mexico? If we had contact with a Mexican patient, why would we think he was Mexican? It cannot be simply because of his name and address, starting from the wrong end, nor by a diagnostic.
> (Bion, quoted by Dupont, 1978, p. 223, my translation)

Bion's emphasizes the value of creativity and imagination as vital; both are the products of what he originally called alpha-function and, later, dreaming. He wrote: "it is so important to dare to think or feel whatever you do think or feel, never mind how un-scientific it is" (Bion, 2014a [1978], p. 211).

In what follows, I intend to address Frida Kahlo's work as a reticular experience in which the meaning of her work can slip through seven oneiric dimensions of the mind or be held in tension between various links. For this purpose, I review the following oneiric dimensions in Frida Kahlo: the familiar, painful, erogenous, social, aesthetic, finite, and infinite. I also attempt to trace some parallels with Bion's contributions, specifically with his masterpiece (Grotstein, 1981) *A Memoir of the Future*.

Last, but not least, I consider that the relation of container-contained and dreaming, beautifully presented by Ogden (2004) addresses this dynamic interaction of the oneiric dimensions of the mind in Frida Kahlo's art. According to Ogden, the contained, like the container, is not a static thing but a *living process* that is continuously expanding and changing (2004, p. 1356). Thus, my invitation to live the different dimensions in Frida Kahlo can also be carried out from Ogden's vertex and from what Bion raised when he wrote:

> Picasso painted on a piece of glass in such a way that it could be appreciated from both sides; the same can be said of the caesura; it depends on which side you look at (Frida); it is the direction in which you are traveling.
> (Bion, 1987, p. 306)

I do not pretend to discover the historical truth, nor do I pretend to recover the unconscious contents of the author's body of work; the methodology is an attempt to generate a movement between the different oneiric dimensions in Kahlo's art.

I will omit in the present work many of the abundant historical and psycho-biographical data that readers can consult in books, such as those of Kahlo's biographers Herrera (1983) and Zamora (1987); I will only use the data that I consider relevant for this presentation. I also assume a certain degree of familiarity with Bion's life and work. I have included what is essential to understanding the work on which the chapter is centered. At the same time, it is probably necessary to state that the following exposition constitutes my dream of Frida Kahlo and Bion's, and it can be seen "from both sides of the screen – both sides of the resistance" (Bion, 1991, p. 465).

In the same way that in *Memoir of the Future* Bion gives voice to his own "multiple selves and personages" (Abel-Hirsch, 2023), I invite you to dream the oneiric dimensions of the mind of the painter that Juan Soriano defined as a woman full of images. Let us evoke Frida to witness that for her, the craft of art was the most direct way to the heart of human sensibility; dreaming (painting), was the primordial form to transform unconscious primordial work with her lived and "unlived experiences" (Ogden, 2019). A phrase from Eekhoff (2024, n.p.): "Familiarity with the primordial never leaves us, but rests silently in our bodies, as background to the truth. We access it in moments of beauty discovered in art, poetry, music, or sexuality".

Lastly, I will include some references as "wild thoughts" (Bion, 1997) but only as a reminder, as in *Hamlet*, to "hold... the mirror up to nature" (III.ii 24–25), to the human condition.

I. Family Oneiric Dimension

The story of Frida Kahlo[3] begins and ends in the same place: in a villa on Calle Londres, in Coyoacán.[4] Her father, Wilhelm (Guillermo) Kahlo, was a Hungarian-German photographer. He had an immense library, played music, and loved painting. He suffered from epileptic seizures from adolescence. He had a first marriage, was widowed, and married Matilde Calderon, an Oaxacan woman described as very religious. These ancestry details took on an exquisite significance for Frida in constructing her own identity, reflecting the complex mixed identity of Mexico after the revolution. On the maternal side, she was of mixed Mexican Spanish and Indigenous descent; on the paternal, she was an immigrant German. Guillermo and Matilde had five children, one of whom died at birth. Two girls were born first (Matilde and Adriana), then, Frida's brother, named Guillermo, who died at birth. Next was Frida, and within two months of her birth, Matilde was pregnant with her fourth daughter, Cristina. Their mother became ill after Cristina's birth and could not feed her; hence, Frida and Cristina were placed at the breast of an Indigenous[5] wet nurse. They both were cared for mainly by their older sisters, Matilde and Adriana, and – whenever they were at home – by their half-sisters María Luisa and Margarita, who had been placed in a convent when their father remarried. Of his six (surviving) children, Frida was the one to whom Guillermo Kahlo felt most attached: he stimulated Frida's intellectual adventurousness.

Like Bion, when he described himself as the "Elephant's Child"[6] (Bion, 2018 [1980], p. 3) for having an insatiable curiosity, Frida had an appetite for learning. These characteristics provided the vital spark for each new story or spiritual journey she undertook.

At the age of six, Frida got sick with poliomyelitis; hence, she and her father were drawn even closer to each other, bound by a shared experience of illness and loneliness. Polio left Frida's right leg skinny and shortened and prone to ulcers and infections that troubled her for decades, leading to an amputation in the final years of her life.

Alone for hours in her bed, a rich interior life emerged, imagining a world beyond the walls; she described her polio experience in her diary as follows:

> Physical immobility left my mind free to glide forward with infinite plans, I turned to my mind as a companion. The fantasy arose that I had an agile imaginary friend who danced as if she were weightless. In one of the passages of my diary, entitled "The Two Fridas", I confessed to having had an imaginary friend whom I jealously guarded for thirty-four years.
>
> (Kahlo 1995, p. 22)

Her dialogue recalls a passage from *A Memoir…*:

MIND: Call me Psyche-Psyche-Soma
BODY: Soma-Psyche
MIND: We must be related
BODY: Never – not if I can help it.(Bion, 1991, p. 433)

We can conjecture that when the body catastrophe of polio occurred, Kahlo found herself dissociate into the warring twins "Psyche and Soma" as a result of her discovering that her "mental membranes" enabled her to reach far beyond her feet. As Ogden (1991) wrote, the body provides a "sensation matrix". In addition, despite Kahlo's polio, her body served as a container for "memories in sensorium" (Eekhoff, 2019).

As a small girl, Kahlo describes herself as a chubby imp. People remembered her with a dimple in her chin and a mischievous glint in her eye (Judah, 2020). These memories illustrate what Eigen (2024) always claims:

> The human psyche does not stop – pulse beats, drum beats, mega and mini-beats, internal-external wars, creativity, interweaving of capacities, mixtures of all sorts with more than dashes of wonder. Real horror is horrible yet we have entertaining horror fiction and art. Whatever disturbs also turns into a myth that structures and magnifies.
>
> (Eigen, 2024, p. 1)

So, as a highly graceful girl who walked (Kettenmann, 2022), she made little jumps so that she seemed to float like a bird in flight. As we will see next, in 1925, this bird turned into a wounded bird.

II. Oneiric Dimension of Pain

The visible impairment of her right leg as a consequence of poliomyelitis did not prevent Kahlo from conceiving life without speed, from climbing trees, from dancing. As a teenager, Kahlo was slender and fragile, with sensitivity and willful energy. She became an oppositional figure, and at the same time, she had a serene and enigmatic performed lightness that made her attractive to the eyes of both men and women. The life of adolescent friendship in the famous intellectually competitive group called "las Cachuchas" was interrupted one afternoon in September 1925 when Kahlo was eighteen. According to Herrera (1983), her biographer, when catching a bus to Coyoacán with Alejandro, her boyfriend, in 1925, a streetcar ran into the bus in which they were traveling; Frida's spine was broken in three places, and her clavicle and two ribs were fractured. Her right leg suffered eleven fractures, and her right foot was dislocated and crushed; her left shoulder was out of place and her pelvis was broken in three places, and the handrail went through her left hip and out through her vagina. The force of the explosion blew her clothes off, and they found her nude, drenched in blood but covered, too, in a gold powder that had exploded out from another passenger's belongings; when people saw her, they cried: "The ballerina, (*la bailarina*)" (Judah, 2020). With the gold of her red, bloody body, they thought she was a dancer (p. 24). The interesting thing (here begins the myth[7]) is that amid this tragedy, spectators of the accident[8] described Kahlo as being "covered with gold dust".

From that day until her death, 29 years later, she lived with pain and the constant threat of illness. She had more than 32 operations and was unable to become a mother; her smashed pelvis led only to miscarriages, and she had three therapeutic abortions. Kahlo flaunted her happiness the way a peacock spreads its tails, but it camouflaged a deep sadness and inwardness, even self-obsession. She was forced to use a plaster corset that served as a prosthesis and had to learn all the lessons of life in a second. As she wrote (Kahlo, 1995): "My friends became women slowly, and I grew old in moments. The desire to become a doctor and live in Europe faded away".

These psychic and biological threats became confusing for the psyche, and anguish acquired catastrophic dimensions; but pain constantly searches for a home and a transformation. In this suffering body with a transgressive aesthetic due to bodily violence, the dislocated images gave rise to new psychic spaces. "I'm not sick; I'm broken", she used to write (Kahlo, 1995).

She faced months of bed rest and isolation. Kahlo's dream of medical school had flown. In the middle of this tragedy, it seems as if Kahlo asked what Bion asked himself after the tank- experiences during the war: "Is there any desert such as a sojourn amongst non-combatants?" (Bion, 1985, p. 52). Kahlo's parents seemed to reply to her human condition; at her mother's suggestion, a carpenter constructed an easel inside her bed frame, allowing her to paint from her frustrating recumbent position. Her father gave her a box of oil colors. This was the beginning of the era of self-portraits. A ray of hope illuminated the room. She wrote in her diary: "We were two Fridas, the one in the mirror and me; from that moment on, my company was myself, I drew lines and gave them a meaning. The paintings acted as balms to my exhausted and aching body" (p. 42).

As the epicenter, the accident broke the alpha chains and triggered vestiges of beta elements to migrate to points of agony. I have found no better words to describe these experiences than what Bion declared in *A Memoir of the Future*: "If somites could write, the book would be interpretations of reality, and the theories would all be what we call dreams" (Bion, 1991, p. 470).

We find more ideas around this theme in the poet John Donne ("The Second Anniversary"): "The blood spoke in her cheeks, and so distinctly wrought, that one might say, the body thought". This illustrates what Bion called B-elements; beta elements are elements not yet transformed but available to the mind (*Brazilian Lectures*, p. 44, emphasis added, in Bion, 2014a). As Bion puts it in *Taming Wild Thoughts*, "Although we tend to have shifted our observations away from the body to the sphere of the mind, the body has not ceased to exist" (1997, p. 44).

To sum up, the well-known phrases "*I do not paint dreams, I paint my reality*" and "*I paint myself because I am the subject I know best*" (Kahlo, 1995) seem an echo of Bion's phrase: "*I write about me*" (Bion, 2014b, p. 8).

To illustrate this oneiric dimension, I close by repeating a statement from *A Memoir of the Future,* where Bion states: "*And please, conscience, go to sleep. The world of reality is your place!*" (1991, p. 99).

III. Erotic Oneiric Dimension

Returning to the *Casa Azul* (Blue House); vivid, intelligent, and sensual, Kahlo attracted men and women. It took some time for Eros to return to her. However, neither the illness, the suffering, nor the accident completely withered her infinite feminine variety; we all know that Kahlo was a woman of the 20th century who left behind the nightgown that covered the bodies of other women and manifested the vicissitudes of her encounters, the struggles and pleasures between her body and those of many men and women. Gods and demons inhabited that body of pain and pleasure. She was seized by the pulsational networks that manifested in the stormy and passionate relationship with Diego Rivera, whom she married when he was 39 and she was 21. In 1929, she became his third wife. During this marriage, she had miscarriages and lost three children. She was particularly innovative in painting the crises of female sexuality, a subject rarely treated with the crudeness she exhibits in paintings such as *My Birth* (1932) and *Henry Ford Hospital* (1932), in which the erotic message was assembled with violence and cruelty.

Again, Kahlo elaborated her sexuality through the subject of her paintings; for instance, she transformed exotic plants into male and female sex organs; the life-giving sun shines down on the phallus, and a fetus emerges from the mother's womb. For the artist, the flower was a symbol of sexuality and feelings. Kahlo's artistic vision here is powerful. There is another vertex we can trace between sexuality and erotism; as Bion made clear in *the Memoir*, sexuality applies to interpersonal relationships and to many other types of cultural meetings where a creative mingling of vertices is required for thought/painting to germinate. It is for this reason (instead of the strictly Freudian) that sexuality, according to Williams (2010b), is the basis of psychoanalytic thinking (p. 18).

IV. Oneiric Aesthetic Dimension[9]

There are numerous studies from the point of view of her pictorial work and abundant myths. Following an aesthetic model[10] inspired by Bion's work, art is not only seen as an activity that fosters sublimation or reparation, or one that provides a space for working our omnipotence. Art is seen fundamentally as a means of favoring new thinking (Abella, 2016, p. 464). Many insightful analysts[11] have variously explored the aesthetic dimension,

Throughout his work, Bion focuses on seeing "constant conjunctions" (Bion, 1965) rather than looking for causal and narrative links and reasoning that are limited to the dimension of psychic functioning. I am interested in highlighting the following themes that I conjecture are present in Kahlo's work.

1 Self-portraits; portraits with friends and animals

Most of the two hundred paintings she produced in her abbreviated career were self-portraits. People who knew her well say Frida's intelligence and humor shone in her eyes (Herrera, 1983). No one is better than Carlos Fuentes (1995) at describing "the era" of self-portraits. The Mexican poet wrote: "The body is the temple of the soul, the face is the temple of the body, and when the body is broken, the soul possesses no more altar than that of a face" (p. 8).

The mirror phase, as a founding moment of the ego, is one of the concepts used to show how the re-editing of this moment, through the gaze into the mirror, concomitantly allowed her to enter the world of painting and attain a narcissistic reorganization through her self-portraits.[12]

2 The disturbing still lives full of suggestions that penetrate through all the senses

She established associations between roots and veins, tendons and nerves, all symbolizing feeding behaviors or ways of pain transmission. The work was anchored in the depths of the body, in the protomental (Bion, 1957). This is reflected, for example, in the painting *Roots* (1943); Frida seemed to be very close to the approaches of Bion's concepts of beta and alfa elements: feeling impressions, passions, common sense, differences between being awake and asleep, the work of the memory and so on.

Painting herself bleeding, weeping, cracked open, she transmuted her pain into art with remarkable frankness tempered by humor and fantasy.

3 The bleeding hearts, as doubles of organs, were part of the duality

She exhibited her open and wounded body, as in the painting *La Columna Rota* (The Broken Spine, 1944). In this painting, we can observe a torso supported by an element of torture, in contrast with the harmonious and intact breast.[13] The corset's straps with metal buckles accentuate the delicate vulnerability of Kahlo's naked breasts – breasts whose perfect beauty makes the rough cut from neck to loins all the more ghastly.

At other times, from that same open human being, life sprang forth as branches carrying blood to fertilize the sterile earth. Like Coatlicue,[14] Khalo embraced the earth with the firmness of a living and permanent plant. With her hips rapped in a cloth, Kahlo displays her wounds like a Christian martyr; as in many of her paintings of suffering, she takes elements of the grizzly rendering of martyrdom – all open wounds, blood, sores, and teardrops – that are a mainstay of Mexican Catholicism.

In what follows I will present some thoughts about the concept of "*caesura*" (Bion, 1989); I find that this concept clearly demonstrates the psychic "habitat" from where Kahlo oscillated. Bion (1965) defined "*caesura*" as a rupture and continuity that shows good and evil, light and darkness. He wonders if a fetus – even in the form of physical pressure in the optic and auditory holes – does not feel the stimulus of the environment in which it is immersed and if marks of blind or embryological intuition cannot persist in postnatal and adult life; in the search for truth, one cannot do without these primitive forms of knowledge, which may sometimes be empty of content but are always waiting for the possibility of being formulated or communicated (Bion 1977, p. 43).

Perhaps, we can conjecture the concept outline above by thinking that Kahlo used the birth of *caesura* as a birth model for each painting. It is worth remembering a passage where Bion (1965) says, "There is, nevertheless, a great deal of functioning continuity before and after the caesura". Following these premises, in Civitarese's (2008) opinion, the text of caesura assumes the meaning of a spiritual testament and uses the caesura of birth as a model of the birth of every thought-dream.

To conclude, I want to consider briefly this phrase; when Bion said:

> I am sure they are embryonic ideas and feelings, primordial ideas that deserve the chance of development. I don't know if they will be good or

bad. Someone will need to have the courage to say: "Even if a monster is born, I will risk giving birth to the child."

(Bion, 2018 [1980], p. 68).

Kahlo illustrates these experiences through all her paintings; each of her paintings produces a "pattern of sound, each with a personality, like a real person" (Bion, 2013 [1967], p. 18). Moreover, when Bion speculates in A *Memoir* on the blush on the walls of the uterus that occurs with the mating of sperm and ovum (Bion 1991, p. 566), and that occurs each time a new idea is conceived, he is re-dreaming the origins of his mind. In another moment, in one painting, details of Kahlo's genesis extend to the very moment her mother's egg is fertilized by her father's sperm, and in both, she is depicted in utero.

V. Social Oneiric Dimension

No description of Kahlo would be complete without mentioning her revolutionary character. Her growth occurred in the context of the years immediately following the Mexican Revolution, a period characterized by a series of artistic, social, and cultural changes coinciding with strong movements in the world, such as surrealism. She had contact with people like Pablo Picasso, Leon Trotsky, and André Breton, with Henry Ford, Nelson Rockefeller, Dolores del Río, and Paulette Goddard. The Rivera home in Mexico was a mecca for the international Pablo Neruda, for Joan Miró and Wassily Kandinsky, all of whom were Kahlo's admirers. The artistic and political expression and the social fabric that she built with Diego Rivera became the mental truth that kept them always close; despite the marital turbulences, what united them were their love for the pre-Hispanic peoples, their political commitment, and their hope for the country, which they maintained until the end. Perhaps the most remarkable facet of this couple was their courage in seeking truth without being preoccupied with results.

Like Rivera, Kahlo wanted her work to show Mexican identity. She was interested in exalting Mexican culture (*lo mexicano*) through the clothes she wore and her paintings. She dressed in flamboyant clothes, greatly preferring floor-length native Mexican costumes to haute couture.

Her identification with the Mexican nation and its cultural roots cannot be seen merely as a portrait of her private surroundings and personal problems. It is an intellectual stance influenced by the political and cultural developments that followed the Mexican Revolution.

VI. Finite Oneiric Dimension

In 1954, Kahlo was convalescing from a lung infection; she participated in a demonstration against the U.S. intervention in Guatemala and, as a consequence, this experience brought serious medical complications. As reflected in the painting The *Wounded Deer* (1946), Kahlo was seriously wounded; she had been trapped by death.

Gradually, the title of the painting *Tree of Hope, Remain Strong* (1946) was replaced by another phrase, *My life is getting dark*. Her health went from bad to worse; she had a continuous feeling of fatigue, and almost constant pain in her spine and right leg damaged so long ago by polio, her right leg became gangrenous, and doctors amputated her leg. In total, Kahlo underwent 30 operations and an encyclopedia of treatment. "She lived dying" said a friend (Herrera, 1983, p. 62).

Kahlo used large amounts of morphine and alcohol in addition to tobacco. Despite her adversities, in all of the paintings one discovers her statement to live life with joy: "I am happy to be alive as long as I can paint" (Kahlo, 1995). Here, she sheds light on what Rezze and Braga (2019) wrote: "We, analysts, feel comfortable with pain and suffering, but only a few of us know what to do when authentic pleasures emerge" (p. 61). She usually painted in bed, and after 1951, she was in such severe pain that she was no longer able to work without taking painkillers. Kahlo always expressed gratitude to Ramon Parres, her psychoanalyst.[15]

In her later years, she wrote a diary (Fuentes, 1995). Like Bion in the third part of *A Memoir*, Kahlo allowed the different ages of herself to dialogue with each other.

Zamora (1987) described Kahlo as an artist of intimacy who collected the brush of anguish and, simultaneously, trapped in her canvases, the brush of the everyday world. The only painting not portrayed was the nocturnal transit to another world (Zamora, 1987, my translation). On July 13, 1954, a pulmonary embolism was diagnosed as the cause of her death. Kahlo was placed in a coffin, and when it closed, it trapped inside all the loneliness that she feared so much; she was accompanied by passion[16] and all the colors of a rainbow life, and although her flame (her life) was extinguished, its sparkles continued to shine.

She lay in state first at Casa Azul; they dressed her like an Aztec princess in all her finery. Then her coffin was placed by a guard of honor in the entrance hall of the Palacio de Bellas Artes and was attended by Diego and former President Lázaro Cardenas.

VII. Infinite Oneiric Dimension

In *A Memoir of the Future*, the pre-born characters, such as *Somita*, have gifts such as contact with the oneiric life. However, the oneiric life also expresses a resistance to being born, that is, to live in the gaseous environment, the shared world where individual renunciations "in favor of the adaptation" are demanded. Kahlo knew how to apprehend the subterranean continuity between the oneiric dimensions; she captured darkness not as an absence of light but as one of its functions. In doing so, she dared to disturb the universe where the different oneiric dimensions acquired a plurality of meanings. Through her brushstrokes, she shared and transformed living emotions into the very place where these emotions could emerge. Among these seven oneiric dimensions, we witness an interplay of multiple movements in the process of dreaming a dream; the Mexican painter invited us to embrace her work through sparks of myth, sense, and passion (Bion, 1963).

I find it reasonable to introduce these ideas in relation to the infinite oneiric dimension of Kahlo, since they connect with Bion's thoughts about vestiges. Just as we can detect "vestiges of the organs of the body", Bion considered, we can speculate that pre-birth functions and post-birth thoughts include *embryonic intuition* (Bion, 1957). He also suggests that the presence of these vestiges can generate creative aspects: "Artists have a great advantage because they can resort to aesthetics as a universal linguistics" (Bion, 2014a [1978]).

Thinking through imaginative conjectures, Bion observed a dynamic prenatal psyche that persists after birth and can be infiltrated into post-natal mental life. Through a series of observations, for Bion, the prenatal psyche remains unintegrated in the post-natal personality and develops after birth through relationships with living objects; "so, when you are dealing with a grown person, you will have to distinguish between something conscious or unconscious and something inaccessible" (Bion 2018, p. 120).

Kahlo's prenatal functioning, vital and with fertile potentialities, is illustrated in the following of Bion's notions: "can we catch the germ of an idea and plant it where it can begin to be developed until it acquires the necessary maturity to be born?" (Bion, 2018 [1980], p. 95). Hence, what is authentic is born from turbulences. As Bion (2014a [1978]) wrote "We can consider artists, musicians, and scientists as those who have been encouraged to lodge transitive thoughts and ideas".

In 2015, Alazraki wrote: "And suddenly a last work appears, vibrant with life, light, color, humidity, full of seeds and with that legend of celebration" (Alazraki, 2015, p. 61, my translation). Eight days before she died, when her hours were darkened by calamity, Kahlo dipped her brush in blood-red paint and inscribed her name, across the crimson pulp of the foremost slice of a watermelon. Then, in large capital letters, she wrote *Viva la Vida*. Alazraki considers that the painting *Viva la Vida* (*Long Live Life*, 1954) functioned as a border between the passage through life and death and left in color the expression of her passage through both.

Bion points out to us a search beyond and even further, from a shapeless infinite into something that may not even be comprehensible but apprehensible, and that may even denote other unknown and new ways. He suggested that we must let emerge from within, depending on the emotional relation aroused, the kind of "artist of life" that exists inside; or, even better, whatever that word "artist" might mean to each of us. For him the artist would find ways of representing the unknown through intuition. Bion states:

You cannot fool your own eyes, making them think there is a tree where there is not. Instead, and much better, you are someone who allows them to see that, in reality, there is a tree there and also its roots, although these are underground (…). I am not simply asking what you see with your eyes, but everything that intuition allows you to see in front of you.
(Bion 2014a, pp. 24–25)

With this in mind, it may be said that in the same way Bion wrote that "O" (1970) is a dark spot that must be illuminated by blindness and that Adam Phillips (2017) said, "If you want to paint a tree, focus on the whole landscape, except the tree", if we want to understand the oneiric dimensions of the mind, let us take a moment with Frida Kahlo and celebrate '*Viva la Vida*, Long Live Life'.

Discussion

We have traversed a long and lively path from the familiar oneiric dimensions of Frida Kahlo, to the infinite dimensions. I was involved in several mental operations that frequently oscillated between one another: forming images, creating stories, and decoding meanings. Each of these activities interlocked tightly with the others. This emotional experience constituted that process that everyone knows is called *reverie*. It was needed to link all these images, connect them, and render them coherent in a narration born as the sum of the product of the various reveries that emerged from this writing. Ogden (2005, p. 1) described this process freshly and subtly as follows "it is my experience that in psychoanalytic writing, as in poetry, a concentration of words and meaning draw on the power of language to suggest what it cannot say"

As Bion recommended in his Paris Seminar (1978), I tried to use all my colors to paint this conversation. Having arrived at our final destination we may now take a brief look back and wonder what we have conjectured through this journey. I will now discuss the ways in which Bion's thinking may help us understand Frida Kahlo's mind.

Although this presentation is arranged chronologically, from "beginnings" in prenatal life to later years, I did not intend to give a reductional view of Frida Kahlo. Kahlo's work opens a way of approaching the ephemeral and ineffable, qualities that seem significant when thinking of the oneiric dimensions of the Mind. She moved toward making "contact with the depths" (Eigen, 2011) –with what Bion, in *Transformations*, named "O" (Bion, 1970). Bion and Kahlo avoid the narrative in their writings/paintings: dialogues are interrupted, and it is not possible to follow a thread or frame it in logic and reason. It is a choral work with many voices. Although there can be a continuity in the names of some paintings-writings, they appear with deep transformations from one moment to another. It is outstanding how both illustrate Eigen's statement "one never recovers from being human" (Eigen, 2011, p. xv).

There are many windows to enter into Kahlo's oneiric dimensions; Bion's text *A Memoir of the Future* is a magnificent Virgil. Page after page, Kahlo brings us from Os to Dantesque regions, purgatories of pain, and then to the paradise of alpha function, container/contained, and reveries. There is a close connection of Kahlo's oneiric dimensions with The *Memoir*, defined by Jenkins (2024) as a catalogue of nightmares, peopled by ghosts. Bion's phrase "These old ghosts, they never die", (Bion, 1989) opened a wider perspective to the readers, unfettering them from the constrains of logical thought. *A Memoir*, as Bion's dreaming of his autobiography, with all its sorrow, horror, and redemption (Grotstein, 1981, p. 7), let him be laid to rest. But to do so would be to forget the men his work immortalizes (Jenkins, 2024).

Another window from which we can enter to capture the oneiric dimensions in Frida Kahlo is through Ogden's rich contribution of the related container-contained. For the author, container-contained is centrally concerned with the processing (dreaming) of thoughts derived from lived emotional experience. He states: "The idea of the container-contained addresses the dynamic interaction of predominantly unconscious thoughts (the contained) and the capacity for dreaming and thinking those thoughts (the container). From this perspective, the capacity for dreaming (the container) requires dream-thoughts; and dream thoughts (the contained) require the capacity for dreaming" facilitating the growth of the container (Ogden, 2004, p. 1359). Ogden always focuses on the intersubjective experience. From this vertex, we might "consider how writing/painting (C/c) is also a way of dreaming oneself into existence" (Ogden, 2004). For Jenkins (2024), for instance, the process of writing and rewriting that Bion underwent with his war memoirs allowed him to create a space in which to reexamine his own experiences. The same goes for Kahlo, who wrote her *Diary* as a central need to let something finite emerge out of the infinity. From another vertex, the painter's canvas, the poet's white page, the composer's ruled sheets, the stage or the ground available to the dancer or the architect, and the film reel, according to Anzieu (2016 [1985]), materialize, symbolize, and revive this experience of the border between the two bodies in symbiosis as a surface of inscriptions, with its paradoxical character – which is found again in the work of art – of being at the same time a surface of contacts.

While Bion rarely explicitly refers to trauma in the body of his theoretical work, for Tarantelli (2016), the narration in his autobiographies of his experiences in the war are "accounts of a psychic catastrophe, a living terror so intense that verbal formulations are inadequate to do it justice". Ferro demonstrates that in trauma, there is a quantitative excess of stimulation of beta-elements, "like a storm of asteroids" (Ferro, 2016, pp. 55–56). It was as if some hidden part of Kahlo managed to keep her body alive despite her "emotional death" in the bus accident. The same goes for Bion and his "emotional death" which occurred with Sweeting's appeal to mediate between his dead self and his mother. Thus, for Kahlo, painting was part of her battle for life.

So, what seems unique is Kahlo's use of her own body, of embodied experiences, despite everything; she provides the means for an unconscious processing of emotions intimately interwoven with the germination of new thoughts.

Another parallel arises between Kahlo and Bion: the former has expressed that she had been writing a diary; as for Bion, almost immediately after his demobilization in 1918, he wrote a diary (Bion, 1997)[17] which was a detailed account of the war. From both experiences, it is evident that the effects were catastrophic. However, their life experiences capture the difference between *remembering an experience* and *becoming the O of that experience.*

The "model of actual physical warfare may be used as a storyline, but the real subject, according to Williams (2010a) is always "the war of the mind, and from that warfare there is no release" (pp. xi–xii). Kahlo also understood this, acknowledging that "death is nothing but a process in order to exist" (Herrera, 1983, p. 421).

In a fantastic paper, Jenkins (2024) considers that *A Memoir of the Future* enables Bion to explore the enduring effects of the war and give representation to his mental states in a way that his more conventional efforts at autobiography do not allow (Jenkins, 2024, p. 10). At the end of their lives, both Bion and Kahlo strove to present not just their life story and not just their thoughts but their mode of thinking in terms of an internal conversation that might be sufficiently realistic in its forms as to become "audible to others" (Bion, 1991, p. 113) Their wish was no other than to dramatize the process of thinking itself; the type of thinking which, however imperfectly, "shapes the thinker", and whose reality is seen in the changing shape of a mind rather than in any theory, message, or summary of experience.

In looking at different paintings of Kahlo's, we witness vertices or parts of a personality communicating with each other, from different ages and points in the evolutions; Williams (2010a, pp. xii–xiii) describes a similar state of mind in Bion's *A Memoir of the Future* in which he traces the complex mind in action, talking from many vertices, from the gamut of his years – the fetus in the womb to the 77-year-old. It presents the living drama of his internal history: amusing, argumentative, profound, puzzling, always unexpected, sometimes blindingly, obviously true. For both, their legacy is the result of the operations carried out by the alpha function in all the perceptual and sensory data in which they were immersed.

One last thought: the body of Bion's work, according to Tarantelli, is a theory of the functioning of the psychotic and traumatized mind. Tarantelli affirms: "Bion was the man who survived the war, and his work is also an attempt to fathom the stupefying fact of aliveness, of the mind [that] is coming into being out of mindlessness and continuing in its existence" (Tarantelli, 2016, p. 61). Hence, both Bion's writings on the war and Kahlo's diary (her most intimate testament) testify to the fragile condition of existence. Their purpose was not to "report" their experiences of the war or the accidents they suffered; instead, perhaps they were attempts to dream the pain of something that remained without being able to be dreamed, unlived (Ogden, 2019). We can read the autobiographical accounts more as a trajectory, an attempt to reach *at-one-ment* with themselves.

"It is so important to borrow the language of painters, musicians and so on, and to use it in this extraordinary subject with which we are concerned", wrote Bion (2014a [1978], p. 203). Rephrasing Bion's words to my convenience: a painter could estimate the quality of the canvas on which to practice his art; a sculptor might discern the grain of the wood or marble which he contemplates; the composer might allow his inner eye to be impinged upon the sight, or his inner ear upon the sounds, from which he chooses to discriminate and then transform into music. In a similar sense, I hope to have succeeded in offering some colors from which we can trace some of the oneiric dimensions of the mind in Frida Kahlo.

To conclude, the seeds have been sown for further dreams and it is time to close by repeating again: *Viva la Vida*, Long Live Life!

Notes

1 Levine for instance, following Freud's theory of representation, conceptualizes these latter forces as "unrepresented" or "weakly represented" (colourless canvas).
2 I was eight years old when my parents took me to visit Frida Kahlo's museum, La Casa Azul. I had contact with the habitat of this icon representative of Mexican culture. I was deeply impacted by the perception of different climates of suffering, desperation, and oneiric that emanated from that rooms of the Blue House; I remember the aroma of poetry and love for nature in the garden, the contrasts and vivid colors of art, history, and folklore of Mexico and the invisible-visible presences of Frida Kahlo and Diego Rivera. Bion's childhood Garden of Eden was India (Williams, 2010a).
3 Her complete name was Magdalena Carmen Frida Kahlo y Calderon.
4 Coyoacán is one of Mexico City's sixteen territorial demarcations located in the city's geographic centre: https://es.wikipedia.org/wiki/Coyoac%C3%A1n
5 Even the detail of her wet nurse played into Frida's origin myth, as seen in a painting titled *My Nurse and I* (1937).
6 This is a reference to Rudyard Kipling's "The Elephant's Child" in *Just So Stories*. In childhood, Wilfred was compared to Kipling's "Elephant Child" and in *All My Sins Remembered* he writes of "Me, the Elephant's Child, one who does not learn for all its questions" (Bion, 1985, p. 51).
7 Using myths and models, Bion finds an original solution that is compatible with the idea of catastrophic change. In category C of the Grid (1965), we use myths to refer to dreams, to our oneiric dimension.
8 Kahlo never painted the accident that broke her body and transformed her from an agile, dancing schoolgirl into a woman who, for the remainder of her life, moved with the maddening red heat of pain. There is a painting called *The Bus*, but it is not the bus that exploded into fragments under the pressure of an oncoming tram, damaging all within it.
9 Biography/chronology: https://www.museofridakahlo.org.mx/frida/?lang=en
   Frida Kahlo Painting:
   https://www.singulart.com/en/blog/2023/10/24/frida-khalo-paintings/?srsltid=AfmBOoocM0lleGnssLRKy8YWswzToeC7EDCp3756SzQ_xVZ-10kT4SuF

10 Since Bion and later Meltzer, the concept of aesthetics has become the essence of the psychoanalytic process.
11 I recommend carefully reading authors who have studied the aesthetic, like Meltzer, Harris, and Pistiner.
12 Knafo (1991) explores the psychoanalytic significance of Egon Schiele's and Frida Kahlo's self-portraits. Both artists employed the self-portrait as a central means of artistic expression.
13 The body-mind relationship also inevitably brings up the possibility of body-mind dissociation (Lombardi, 2017, p. 6). Lombardi is also quite particular in drawing his ideas from early work in Bion on the body and somatic states.
14 The mighty Aztec mother goddess Coatlicue wears a skirt of snakes. Her slack breasts are garlanded with hearts, several hands, and a skull emanating from her waistband. She is the deity both of childbirth and of death, of creation and destruction: a forbidding reminder that birth launches the soul on a journey with one particular ending. The duality embodied by Coatlicue maintains balance in the universe. There can be no life without death, chaos without order, rebellion without conformity (Judah, 2020, p. 9).
15 Ramón Parres was a pioneer of the Mexican Psychoanalytic Association. He trained in New York City and was analyzed by Sandor Rado. Dr. Parres was also my father's analyst.
16 Kahlo has been defined as a woman with "passion", considering passion to be a very intense emotion. However, according to Meltzer, passion represents a state of turbulence derived from the conflict between newly evolving emotions and mind states and old residual organizations of our internal world (Miggliozzi, 2016).
17 Bion's autobiographical narratives *A Memoir of the Future* (1975–1979) and *The Long Week-End* (1982), together with its sequel *All My Sins Remembered* (1985), are the key to his self-analysis of internal grouping and their shifting patterns. *A Memoir of the Future*, therefore, represents the most finely honed examples of his teaching method.

References

Abel-Hirsch, N. (2023). *Bion, an Introduction*. Phoenix House.
Abella, A. (2016). Using art for the understanding of psychoanalysis and using Bion for the understanding of contemporary art. In H. Levine and G. Civitarese (eds.), *The W. R. Bion Tradition. Lines of Development*. Karnac.
Alazraki, S. (2015). Viva la vida: Frida Kahlo. *Transiciones Psicoanalíticas: Revista de Analistas en Formación de la Asociación Psicoanalítica Mexicana*, 2, 61–68.
Anzieu, D. (2016). *The Ego Skin*. Karnac. (Original work published 1985.)
Bergstein, A. (2013). Transcending the Caesura: Reverie, Dreaming and Counter-Dreaming. *International Journal of Psychoanalysis*, 94(4), 621–644.
Bion, W.R. (1957). *Experiences in Groups*. Tavistock.
Bion, W.R. (1963). *Elements in Psychoanalysis*. Basic Books.
Bion, W.R. (1965). *Transformations: Change from Learning to Growth*. Karnac.
Bion, W.R. (1970). *Attention and Interpretation*. Tavistock.
Bion, W.R. (1977). Emotional turbulence. In P. Hartocollis (ed.), *Borderline Personality Disorders* (pp. 3–15). International Up.
Bion, W.R. (1985). *All My Sins Remembered*. Karnac.
Bion, W.R. (1987). *Clinical Seminars and Four Papers*. Fleetwood. (Original work published 1976.)

Bion, W.R. (1989). Caesura. In *Two Papers: The Grid and Caesura* (pp. 35–56). Karnac. (Original work published 1977.)
Bion, W.R. (1990). *Brazilian Lectures.* Karnac. (Original work published 1974.)
Bion, W.R. (1991). *A Memoir of the Future.* Karnac.
Bion, W.R. (1997). *Taming Wild Thoughts.* Routledge.
Bion, W.R. (2005). *The Tavistock Seminars.* Karnac.
Bion, W.R. (2013). *Los Angeles Seminars and Supervision.* Routledge. (Original work published 1967.)
Bion, W.R. (2014a). A Paris Seminar 1978. In *The Complete Works of W.R. Bion.* Routledge. (Original work published 1978.)
Bion, W.R. (2014b). The Long Weekend 1897–1919: Part of a Life. In *The Complete Works of W.R. Bion.* Routledge. (Original work published 1982.)
Bion, W.R. (2018). *Bion In New York and Sao Paulo.* The Harris Meltzer Trust. (Original work published 1980.)
Civitarese, G. (2008). 'Caesura' as Bion's Discourse on Method. *International Journal of Psychoanalysis*, 89, 1123–1143.
Civitarese, G. and Ferro, A. (2015). *The Analytic Field and its Transformations.* Karnac.
Dupont, M.A. (1978). Algunas impresiones sobre Wilfred R. Bion y texto de una entrevista. *Cuadernos de Psicoanálisis*, 11(3/4), 212–225.
Eekhoff, J.K. (2019) *Trauma and Primitive Mental States: An Object Relations Perspective.* London and New York: Routledge.
Eekhoff, J.K. (2024). *Bion's Emotional Links: Love, Hate & Knowledge.* Routledge.
Eigen, M. (2011). *Contact with Depth.* Karnac.
Eigen, M. (2024). *Bits of Psyche.* Routledge.
Ferro, A. (1999). *The Bi-personal Field: Experiences in Child Analysis.* Routledge. (Original work published 1992.)
Ferro, A. (2008). *Reveries. An Unfettered Mind.* Eulama International Library Agency.
Ferro, A. (2016). Commentary on Levy and Finnegan. *Journal of the American Psychoanalytic Association*, 64, 55–62.
Ferro, A. (2019). *Psychoanalysis and Dreams: Bion, the Field and the Viscera of the Mind.* Routledge.
Freud, S. (1961). *Letters of Sigmund Freud 1873–1939.* Hogarth.
Fuentes, C. (1995). *Introducción en el Diario de Frida Kahlo.* La Vaca Independiente.
Grotstein, J. (ed.). (1981). *Do I dare disturb the universe? A Memorial to Wilfred R. Bion.* Caesura Press.
Herrera, H. (1983). *Frida: A Biography of Frida Kahlo.* Harper Perennial.
Jenkins, T. (2024). "These old ghosts, they never die": The enduring experience of the First World War in Bion's late literary and autobiographical writing. Paper presented at the Bion Commemoration Conference on July 7, 2024.
Judah, H. (2020). *Frida Kahlo. Lives of the Artists.* Laurence King Publishing.
Kahlo, F. (1995). *El Diario de Frida Kahlo. Un íntimo autorretrato.* Debate.
Kettenmann, A. (2022). *Frida Kahlo.* Taschen.
Knafo, D. (1991). Egon Schiele and Frida Kahlo: The Self-Portrait as Mirror. *Journal of the American Academy of Psychoanalysis*, 19(4), 630–647.
Levine, H. (2012). The Colourless Canvas: Representation, Therapeutic Action and the Creation of Mind. *International Journal of Psychoanalysis*, 93(3), 607–629.

Lombardi, R. (2017). *Body-Mind Dissociation in Psychoanalysis. Development After Bion*. Routledge.

Miggliozzi, A. (2016). Passion. In H. Levine and G. Civitarese (eds.), *The W. R. Bion Tradition: Lines of Development*. Karnac.

Ogden, T.H. (1991). *Some Theoretical Comments on Personal Isolation. Psychoanalytic Dialogues*, 1(3), 377–390.

Ogden, T. (2004). On Holding and Containing, Being and Dreaming. *International Journal of Psychoanalysis*, 85(6), 1349–1364.

Ogden, T. (2005). *This Art of Psychoanalysis: Dreaming Undreamt Dreams and Interrupted Cries*. Routledge.

Ogden, T. (2019). Reclaiming Unlived Life: Experiences in Psychoanalysis. *International Journal of Psychoanalysis*, 95, 1–196.

Ogden, T. (2022). *Coming to Life in the Consulting Room. Toward a New Analytic Sensibility*. Routledge.

Phillips, A. (2017). Workshop Winnicott. New Center for Psychoanalysis, Los Angeles.

Pistiner, L. (2009). *The Aesthetic Dimension of the Mind. Variations on a Theme of Bion*. Karnac.

Rezze, C.J. and Braga, J. (2019). Authentic Pleasure: Capture of Moments of Unison with Reality. In A. Alisobhani and G. Corstorphine (eds.), *Explorations in Bion's 'O': Everything We Know Nothing About*. Routledge.

Sandler, P.C. (2005). *The Language of Bion: A Dictionary of Concepts*. Karnac.

Santamaria, J. (2018). D. Winnicott y W. Bion en la clinica: un dialogo com Frida Kahlo. In W. Cidade, C. Cerezer, N. Gonçalves, A. Magalhães, A. Melgaço. & R. Rojas (orgs.), *Winnicott: Integração e Diversidade*. Prospectiva.

Snell, R. (2023). *Antonino Ferro. An Introduction*. Karnac.

Tarantelli, C. B. (2016). "I shall be blown to bits": Towards Bion's Theory of Catastrophic Traumas. In H. Levine and G. Civitarese (eds.), *The W. R. Bion Tradition. Lines of Development*. Karnac.

Williams, M.H. (2010a). *Bion's Dream. A Reading of the Autobiographies*. Karnac.

Williams, M.H. (2010b). *The Aesthetic Development: The Poetic Spirit of Psychoanalysis: Essays on Bion, Meltzer, Keats*. Karnac.

Zamora, M. (1987). *El pincel de la angustia*. Martha Zamora.

Chapter 12

Beatriz and *The Great Mystical Circus*
The Musical and Poetical Transformation of an Emotional Experience

Raul Hartke and Edu Martins

"Beatriz" is the centerpiece of the musical *O Grande Circo Místico* ("The Great Mystical Circus"), written in 1983 for Ballet Teatro Guaíra, a dance company from Curitiba, Brazil. The song was written by Edu Lobo, with lyrics by Chico Buarque de Holanda (Lobo and Buarque, 1983). Naun Alves de Souza, the screenwriter, came up with the concept of the musical inspired by the poem of the same name by Jorge de Lima from 1938 (Lima, 1938). The poem tells the story of the love between the son of Austrian Empress Maria Theresa's court physician and a circus acrobat named Agnes. After watching her performance, the young man falls in love with her, they get married, he abandons his plan of becoming a doctor, and the couple gives rise to the dynasty behind the world-renowned "Grand Circus Knieps".

In Buarque's lyrics, Agnes becomes Beatriz, a circus ballerina. (The lyrics in Portuguese are available at https://tinyurl.com/269kt5db.)

In our opinion, the other songs in the musical, all written by Lobo and Buarque, express, through other characters and storylines, emotions stemming from the same experience contained and transformed musically and poetically in "Beatriz".

We believe that with "Beatriz", Lobo and Buarque achieved a singularly fertile integration between lyrics and music as the non-verbal language of emotion (Juslin, 2013, 2019; Juslin and Sloboda, 2010; Meyer, 1956; Huron, 2007). This integration can sensorially transform, as Bion would put it, as much as possible, the impact of a significant emotional experience, even if it remains, as always, ineffable in its essence.

We will comment on the song from the vertex of Donald Meltzer's theory of the aesthetic object (Meltzer and Williams, 1988), deeply rooted in Bion's work, looking to detail the musical and lyrical technical resources used to convey the emotions experienced (Bion, 1970). We suggest listening to the original recording, performed by Milton Nascimento, available on streaming services.

We consider this song a particularly successful example of the *"language of achievement"* (Bion, 1970).

According to Meltzer, the aesthetic object is one (primarily the mother) with a beautiful exterior, perceptible by sense organs, and an essentially mysterious interior, which can only be approximately conceived by creative imagination. The impact of that object triggers emotional love, hate, and knowledge links (Bion's L, H, and K links), along with their negative links. described by Meltzer as puritanism (-L), hypocrisy (-H), and philistinism (-K) (Meltzer and Williams, 1988).

"Beatriz", divided into four sections or parts, uses the AABA format, with a brief intro and a similarly brief finale. The composer himself has made the original score available at the link: https://edulobo.com.br/wp-content/uploads/2017/11/Beatriz.pdf.

The intro, played on an unaccompanied piano, forms a sequence with a descending melodic contour. The last two chords make up a "plagal cadence", which elicits a sense of calm, stress-free resolution. In "Beatriz", this contrasts with the unsettling early lines of the song, thus intensifying its impact.

The first A section, like all others, begins with a call out from the main character—the young man who, at this point, is still training to be a physician—for us to join him in admiring Beatriz. "*Look*", he says. In other words, he invites us to use our visual perception to observe the fascinating ballerina.

However, the enamored spectator immediately begins expressing a disturbing sequence of questions, doubts, uncertainties, and suspicions. This is why the following four lines are questions beginning with the word "será", an "is she" or "is it" structure. Is she a damsel? Is she sad? Is it the other way around? Is her face a painting, i.e., just a mask hiding her true self? That last idea suggests a first defensive retreat when faced with a disturbing aesthetic impact.

At the same time, the melody now evolves into an ascending shape. This ascending melodic motion causes an experience similar to the physical motion of going up toward something or someone, as demonstrated by the research conducted by musicologist Steve Larson. From the perspective of embodied cognition, Arnie Cox, another musicologist, puts forth the hypothesis of "physical mimetism", which makes the listener feel the song in their body rather than just hear it. We consider that these sensations at the corporal level are transformed into idiosyncratic psychic experiences thanks to the alpha function.

In musical terms, at the moment the letter "O" in "Olha" ("Look") is sung, the composer uses a chord with two tritones. A tritone is composed of three whole tones between two notes. Known as *diabolous in musica*, its use was forbidden in medieval liturgical music. It is the most unstable interval in Western music, a source of tension, disquiet, expectation, and desire, requiring some sort of resolution. Pianist and psychoanalyst Julie Jaffee Nagel

(2013) calls it a "… sonic metaphor for ambiguity, restlessness, and instability" (p. 34).

Consequently, the two-tritone chord works to trigger these emotions. Lahdelma and Eerola (2016), musicologists, demonstrate that single chords, regardless of whether they belong to a harmonic sequence, can effectively convey specific emotional qualities.

In addition, in the case of "Beatriz", the chord is outside the tonal center of the harmony, further increasing the tension.

To us, these elements come together to suggest the restlessness typical of the impact of an aesthetic object, as described by Meltzer and Williams (1988); an emotional turbulence, in the words of Bion.

The chord sequence accompanying the "*serás*" also forms an ascending line, thus enhancing the feeling of climbing towards something, which is also conveyed by the melodic line.

The next four lines in that first verse use the "what if" question structure. The first two ask if Beatriz dances in seventh heaven and if she believes that's another country. Seventh heaven is the symbol of total and complete happiness in medieval Christianity and Islam. However, the term seems to allude more immediately to the "sphere of the contemplatives" in Dante Alighieri's *Divine Comedy*, since Beatrice, the embodiment of faith, is the one who leads the poet to the doors of the Empyrean. At the time the song was written, the term was also the name of a gossip magazine focusing on Brazilian soap opera stars of the '70s and '80s. Therefore, is Beatriz a beatific heavenly creature, or just hungry for fame?

The melody, still with an ascending contour, reaches the song's highest note precisely when the word "*céu*" ("heaven") is sung out, i.e., when the height of beatitude is achieved. It stays there while the lyrics allude to the chance Beatriz might believe it is another country. Next, it descends rapidly while the song questions if she might not simply be memorizing her role, a charming presence on stage rather than being authentic, genuine, and real. Maybe she is just a beautiful actress! Maybe she is a seductive "Blue Angel" in a rundown dance club (like in "The story of Lily Braun", another song in the musical) and the dazzled audience member becomes the clown with "*a broken heart*," a "*human rag*" destined to die backstage, like in "Waltz of Clowns". The harmonic sequence follows the same descent. Everything seems to fall apart, to fall down!

Here, then, we see emerge the desire to know her interior, to answer every question, uncertainty, and suspicion, to resolve this emotional turbulence: "What if I could come into her life?". But Beatriz remains in her world, distant, inaccessible, secretive, mysterious. In the song, "About All Things", the young man expresses intense sorrow that his love is unrequited:

> For God's sake, can't you see that it's a sin, to scorn who loves you so… Is the God who created our desire as cruel as that? He shows us the valleys of

milk and honey, and these valleys are things from God... Can't you see God gets mad when someone is forsaken...?

Meltzer and Williams (1988) underscore that the reciprocity of the object in terms of aesthetic impact is key to contain the emotional turbulence and for the emotional disposition to know (i.e., the K link) to predominate over the other links. The K link, in turn, implies sufficient tolerance to the permanent and unavoidable sense of uncertainty and infinitude.

In "Beatriz", the desire for intruding into the aesthetic object supposedly in order to unveil its mystery and thus control it, remains as such, i.e., just a yearning. But the force of that yearning for violent intrusion, for violating their privacy, in Meltzer's words (Meltzer and Williams, 1988), is evident in the song "Beauty and the Beast", also from this musical, sung in Tim Maia's famously booming voice. In it, a wild and rude man, who describes himself as the strongest man on the planet, as *"Superman"* who can *"tie rails in knots"* and *"eats roller bearings for lunch"*, says: *"Oh, beauty, bring out the spring, wave your magic wand. Oh, beauty, turn the awful beast into a Christian prince. Receive your poet, oh, beauty. Open up your heart or I'll break in through the window"* Significantly, in that same sense, the line "*What if I could come into her life?*" ends every verse of "Beatriz".

The section ends with a so-called dominant chord, which contains a tritone. Consequently, it causes restlessness and tension, requiring some form of resolution, which does not happen within the verse.

The next section has the same melody and harmony as the previous one. The lyrics, however, differ. New questions are asked with each line. It also concludes with the same desire to penetrate the mysterious privacy of the muse (*"What if I could come into her life?"*).

Is Beatriz's home, her life, made out of china? Is it made out of ether, that rapidly evaporates, an anesthetic to dull the senses? Actually, the word "aesthetics" comes from the Greek *aisthesis*, meaning sense perception, bypassing reason.

At this point, it also manifests itself in the fear of losing one's mind, of going mad: *"Is it madness?"*. What if the actress's home is just scenery, something unreal? Would that represent an expression of foreseeing intense psychic turbulence, which, according to Bion, follows a "catastrophic change", that is, a violent internal transformation caused by the sudden subversion of the personality's previous status quo? In this case, that transformation would lead the young lover to abandon medical school and a future life as a physician for the local aristocracy to run a circus and marry a ballerina. After all, in the words of "The Mystical Circus", *"I don't know if it's a new illusion, if there's reincarnation after a deadly somersault"*. Keep in mind that the chords coinciding with each "*será*" ("is it" or "is she") promote a sense of confusion.

The lines beginning with "*e se?*" (what if?) are once again sung at the highest level of the melodic and harmony ascent. Now, however, "*céu*" (meaning both "heaven" and "sky") turns into "*arranha-céu*" (skyscraper). Not only that, this skyscraper might be an illusion, with walls made out of chalk that can be easily erased. This transformation, therefore, falls from heavenly idealization to mundane illusion, followed by disillusionment – "What if she cries in a hotel room?" – the latter coinciding with the suddenly descending contour of melody and harmony, working as a gravitational pull downward. The motion tends to elicit a sense of sadness, metaphorically expressed, for instance, in the expression "to fall into depression", as proposed by Larson (2012).

At the same time, we can conjecture that this disillusionment, even if a source of distress, represents a devaluation of the object as an additional defense. The emotional turbulence caused by the aesthetic impact would not be as strong if Beatriz was only an illusion, or a lonely woman, crying in a hotel room by herself, rather than a stunning ballerina. This defensive retreat is even more evident in another song from the musical *A Ciranda da Bailarina* ("The Ballerina's Nursery Rhyme"), suggestively sung by a children's choir. As if to say that "the emperor has no clothes," they sing that

> *If you look for it, everyone has a sore, a pockmark or vaccine scar. They have the runs ... a mole...athlete's foot... bad manners... lice... gunk in their eye... fear of going up... of going down... vertigo... sin... dirty behind the ear... old panties... family trouble... Only the ballerina doesn't?*

That last question summarizes an attempt to de-idealize the aesthetic object, even if only in the form of a series of questions that cannot ultimately shatter the illusion.

As a defensive reaction to these growing uncertainties and the fear of disillusionment, it returns to the desire for intrusion ("*What if I could come into her life?*") sung over the disquieting dominant chord.

The B section then begins unlike the A sections both in lyrics and in harmony. In it, the spectator sings out an affirmative "*sim*" (yes). In love, he asks the muse to take him with herself forever ("*para sempre*"), teaching him "not to walk with [his] feet on the ground". In other words, even if he can't know or control Beatriz's interior, the lover wants to be taken by her to an impossibility every lover wants regardless, that is, eternity. At the same time, this *not walking with his feet on the ground*—imagining, dreaming—leads the ecstatic lover to write poetry and compose music, for instance.

As for the music, the change in lyrics is accompanied by a change in tonality. It should be stressed that major tonalities always convey more open, more enlightened, even more triumphant sensations. A minor key, in turn, conveys sadder, darker, more closed-off feelings. In this part of the song, the modulation shifts into a minor key. However, the composer uses a sophisticated element to disguise the minor key, known as a *chord extension*, with the goal of creating a false sense of triumph and affirmation. This is the reason the affirmative "*sim*" (yes), so illuminating, is affectively felt with some of the melancholy typical of minor tones even by listeners unfamiliar with music theory, as shown by recent research (Lahdelma and Eerola, 2015).

The melodic contour is also different from the A sections. In this B section, after "*sim*" (yes) is sung over the ambiguous chord, the contour oscillates much more. After a brief initial "depression," exactly accompanying the line "*take me forever*", there is an ascent, with the muse's name sung out in the highest note. In other words, the desire is to ascend with her to a heavenly sphere, but "forever" has a descending nonverbal base, i.e., melody. This means there is also ambiguity between melody and lyrics at this moment.

The next line sounds even more significant in this aspect. The singer asks Beatriz to teach them "*not [to] walk with my feet on the ground*", that is, to let imagination soar, to dream and wonder, singing over a descending melodic line, with the word "*chão*" (ground) coinciding with the lowest note in the whole song. This is the moment where the melody brings the listener back to earth, metaphorically working as a gravitational force, according to Larson (2012), opposing the detachment of loving dreams.

The next line repeats the initial melodic descent in "forever". In the succeeding ascending line, the word "*triz*" (from "*por um triz*", a close call) is sung with the same note as *Beatriz* in the first verse, thus placing that foreboding sense of risk and danger at the same level of importance as the muse's name. It should be stressed that the word "*triz*" is part of the name Beatriz. Therefore, the risk that this utopia might crumble is present in the beautiful actress. This means that there are lyrical and musical cues acknowledging the unsustainable permanence of that "*forever*" for which lovers yearn.

The next two lines proceed with the same fears and uncertainties. The spellbound young man sees in Beatriz a gypsy who could tell his fortune, asking her about future disasters in the palm of his hand and if there is danger in happiness. The first line begins with a painful "*Ai*" (Oh), accompanied by the verse's highest note, one tone above that corresponding to "*Beatriz*" and to "*triz,*" as if representing the moment of maximum distress. Both lines follow a descending contour, pressing downward, until the verse ends with the word "*feliz*" (happy) when questioning "*if it's dangerous for us to be happy*". This anguished question is reinforced by the fact that "*feliz*" (happy) is sung over the same chord finishing each section, which, as discussed previously, serves to convey tension.

The last section has melody and harmony like the first two; the lyrics are different once again, but persist with questions, this time on a heavenly and universal level. Is the beautiful actress a star, shining in the night sky, like love in a sad soul, but unreachable? And the doubts, uncertainties, and insecurities about her true nature return: is her life a lie, a comedy, or divine?

With the last words, the reference to Dante's *Divine Comedy* and his muse becomes evident. Next, at the melody's highest level, another disturbing expression of the fear of disappointment: "*What if she falls out of the sky one day? What if the audience asks for an encore?*". In other words, what if reality suddenly shows it's all an act, nothing but theater? What if the muse reveals herself to be just a beautiful actress, who, like a sorceress or a siren, fascinates the whole audience and drives men mad? But a countervailing hope reappears as well, manifesting in the line about an archangel passing the hat around for tips. That last expectation is paradoxically sung over the familiar descending line, expressive of a fall. Therefore, desire and reality do battle within the lover, playing the highest and lowest strings of their emotions, sparking a series of consonances and dissonances in their mind.

The last line is the same used to close out each verse, i.e., the desire to come into Beatriz's life and unveil her mysterious intimacy. As told in Lima's original poem (Lima, 1938) the young man marries Beatriz and starts a circus family with her. This narrative is equally clear throughout the musical. However, the other songs also make it evident that passions, conflicts, distress, and defenses generated by the impact of the aesthetic object will persist, requiring continence.

The song ends with the same melody and harmony as the introduction, but with the addition of string instruments and the singer humming along with the melody. Strings are particularly effective at conveying emotion, especially nostalgia, sadness, and tenderness, perhaps due to the similarity between their timbres and features of the human voice (Juslin and Västfjäll, 2000; Lahdelma and Eerola, 2015, 2016).

The harmony concludes with plagal cadence, a harmonic modulation that promotes the sense of coming home, to a calm, stable, balanced, and stress-free environment. It's often used in church music, in hymns ending with the word "Amen". In religious tradition, "Amen" means "so be it".

The melody at this point features a descending sequence ending with a so called major third. In melodies, the major third also conveys a strong sense of homecoming, familiarity, and welcoming, often metaphorically associated with the mother and the return to one's mother's arms. For all of these reasons, the emotion elicited at the end matches that of someone who has left their habitual psychic state and now returns to it with more "strings", i.e., more resources to express their emotions. Both the music and the singer's calm intonation suggest, at least to us, a state of *reverie*. Subtly, almost inaudibly, the piano in the background plays the final notes, a sweet ascending line from low to highest, absent from the intro. It is as if, in that state of *reverie*, musician and lyricist internally take their feet off the ground and start to fly, to dream, and turn into a hummingbird, like in "The Mystical Circus", another song in the musical: "*So many flowers rain that, unreflectingly, an ardent spectator turns into a hummingbird*". It is that tiny bird that flaps its wings and kisses a flower, the beautiful actress Beatriz.

Good reveries for all of us.

REFERENCES

Alighieri, D. *A Divina Comédia: Paraíso*. Edição Bilingue. Trad. Ítalo Eugenio Mauro, 4th ed. São Paulo: Editora 34.
Bion, W.R. (1970). *Attention and Interpretation*. Tavistock.
Cox, A. (2017). *Music and Embodied Cognition: Listening, Moving, Felling and Thinking*. Bloomington: Indiana University Press.
Huron, D. (2007). *Sweet Anticipation: Music and Psychology of expectation*. Cambridge/London: MIT Press.
Juslin, P. N. (2013). What does music express? Basic emotions and beyond. *Frontiers in Psychology*, 4, pp. 1–14.
Juslin, P. N. (2019). *Musical Emotions Explained*. Oxford: Oxford University Press.
Juslin, P. N. and Västfjäll, D. (2008). Emotional responses to music: the need to consider underlying mechanisms. *Behavioral and brain Sciences*. 31, p. 559–621.
Juslin, P. N. and Sloboda, J. A. (2010). *Handbook of Music and Emotion: Theory, Research, Applications*. New York: Oxford University Press.
Lahdelma, I. and Eerola, T. (2015). Theoretical proposals on how vertical harmony may convey nostalgia and longing in musica. *Empirical Musicology Review*. 10, 3, pp. 245–263.
Lahdelma, I. and Eerola, T. (2016). Single Chords convey distinct emotional qualities to both näive and expert listeners. *Psychology of music*. 44, 1, pp. 37–54.
Larson, S. (2012). *Musical Forces: Motion, Metaphor, and Meaning in Music*. Bloomington: Indiana University Press.
Lima, J. (1938). A Túnica Inconsútil. In: *Anunciação e encontro de Mira-Celi*. Rio de Janeiro: Record.
Lobo, E., and Buarque, C. (1983). *O Grande Circo Místico*. Rio de janeiro: Som Livre.
Meltzer, D. and Williams, M. H. (1988). *The apprehension of beauty*. Strath Tay: Clunie Press.
Meyer, L. B. (1956). *Emotion and Meaning in Music*. Chicago: The University of Chicago Press.
Nagel, J. J. (2013). *Melodies of the Mind: Connections between Psychoanalysis and Music*. London/New York: Routledge.

Index

Note: Page numbers followed by "n" refer to notes.

"About All Things" 138–139
Abraham 102
aesthetic object 16, 122, 124–126, 136–139
affect management 9, 29
Alazraki, S. 128
Alighieri, D. 138, 142
All My Sins Remembered (Bion) 132n6, 133n17
Al-Muqayyar, Iraq 102
alpha function/elements 8, 25, 27, 29, 49, 58–59, 125, 137; narratives 9; transformations 56; visual images 9
altered consciousness 53
analysts 27–28, 63; act of interpretation 28; dream-work-alpha 98–99; as a dream-worker 49; experiencing mental pain 97–98; four groups of factors in personality of 97–101; inductive function 58; intuition and (*see* intuition); oneiric dimensions (*see* oneiric dimensions of mind); personal myths 100–101; reverie function 99, 105n3; unconscious 63
analytic session 90–95; conceptual level 93–94; observations 92; ultimate reality 71–73
Anzieu, D. 109, 130
Aristotle 4, 6, 8, 26, 30n4
art: as a means of favoring new thinking 124; as a pleasurable entertainment 117; *see also* painting
Artemidorus 17n2
artistic models 117, 124
A-Santamaría Psychoanalysis Mexico Association AC 2
assertive statements 40

attention 52, 86
Attention and Interpretation (Bion) 17n3, 30n3, 45
austere models 40

Baudelaire, C. 68n3
"Beatriz" 16, 136–142; ascending melodic motion 137, 138; sections/parts 137; "what if" question structure 138
"Beauty and the Beast" 139
beliefs 103
Bernard, E. 109, 110
beta function/elements 12, 24, 27, 34, 50, 58–59, 123, 125, 130; alpha function transforming 58–59; as sensorial sensations 9; as unprocessed data 9
beta screen 25, 58
Beyond the Pleasure Principle (Freud) 6
Bion, P. 2
Bion, W. R. 2–3, 8–17; *All My Sins Remembered* 132n6, 133n17; *Attention and Interpretation* 17n3, 30n3, 45; autobiographical narratives 131, 133n17; binocular vision 113; catastrophic change 132n7, 139; *Cogitations* 8, 10, 86–87, 100, 114; communication for 118; death of 2, 11; dreams/dreaming for (*see* dreams/dreaming, Bion's theory of); *Elements* 85; emotional death 130; *The Italian Seminars* 95; as a landscape painter 108; *Language and the Schizophrenic* 47–48; *Learning from Experience* 2, 8, 42; *The Long Week-End 1897–1919* 133n17; 'Memory and Desire' 39; *A*

Memoir of the Future 10, 16, 17n14, 23, 75, 108, 114, 118–121, 123, 127, 130–131, 133n17; model of zones 84–89; Monteiro on 11, 13, 15, 17n12; myths and models 132n7; *Oneiric Dimensions of the Mind* 2; Paris Seminar 129; 'The Psycho-Analytic Study of Thinking' 40; Poincaré and 47; sexuality for 124; suffering for 43–47; tank experiences 122–123; *Taming Wild Thoughts* 123; 'Theory of Thinking' 39, 40, 41; *Transformations* 15, 85, 90, 111, 117, 129; Wittgenstein and 39–43, 47–48
Blanchot, M. 114
Blass, B. R. 5, 17n7
Bleger, J. 56
Braga, J. 10–11, 127
Breuer, J. 6
Brown, L. 18n19
Buarque, C. 16, 136
Buber, M. 30n2

caesura 125
catastrophic change 132n7, 139
Cézanne, P. 15, 107–114; coloured touches 110, 111; Danchev on 108, 114; sensations 108–112
A Ciranda da Bailarina 140
Civitarese, G. 56, 108, 125
Coatlicue 125, 133n14
Cogitations (Bion) 8, 10, 86–87, 100, 114
Cohen, K. 17n14
communication 25, 92, 118
condensation 5, 28
conscious/consciousness 12, 29, 85; altered 53; dream-ready state 56; *see also* oneiric dimensions of mind
constant conjunctions 86, 103, 124
construct 102, 105n2
container-contained 16, 119, 130
COVID-19 2
Cox, A. 137
cross purposes 44

Danchev, A. 108, 114
day-dreams/day-dreaming 12, 50–58; aim of 51; analysis 55–57; collective experience 54–55; defensive dissociation *vs.* 50; dreaming-while-asleep *vs.* 51–53; dysfunction 55; erotism and pleasure 51; as facilitating environment 54; failure 57–58; function 52–53; hypnoid mechanisms 52; mental function 53; reality principle orientation 52; virtual realities 54–55
day's residue 4, 5, 8
"Death Pit of the Royal Cemetery of Ur" 97, 101–105
Deleuze, G. 85
de Souza, N. A. 136
diameter of the circle 71, 72, 75–80
displacement 5, 28
distortion 61
Donne, J. 123
dream-ready state 56
'Dreams and Occultism' (Freud) 42
dreams/dreaming, Bion's theory of 8–11, 32–37; affect management 9; as an emotional experience 8–9; being awake 8; Ferro on 9; as full-time ongoing psychic activity 8, 29; Grotstein on 11, 22–30; hologram 9; normative psychic functioning 24; Ogden on 9; real change and development 11
dreams/dreaming, Freud's theory of 27–28; as an expression of intrapsychic conflicts 6; component operations 4–5; excitation 4; Ferro on 9; functions and meanings 7; interpretation 5–6; molecular method 6; as nighttime event 8, 11; Ogden on 9; primary processes 4–5, 27, 28; as a psychic act 3–4; regressive character 4; secondary process 5; stimulus 4; theory of 1, 3; as thinking 6; tripartite structural theory 6
dream-work-alpha 49, 98–99
drives, daydreaming and 51

Eekhoff, J. K. 120
Eerola, T. 138
ego 6; adaptive function 6; mirror phase 124; unconscious 84
Eigen, M. 10, 17n14, 121, 129
Elements (Bion) 85
Eliot, T. S. 86, 114
embodied cognition 137
embryonic intuition 128
emotion/emotional experiences 8, 12, 85, 93–94; sense impressions 9, 29; transformation 71–72; unconscious 61
emotional turbulence 80, 138–139, 140

empiricism 73–74
Eshel, O. 93

failure to day-dream 57–58
female sexuality 123–124
Ferro, A. 8–10, 11, 15, 65, 105, 108, 110, 113, 115, 118, 130; visual images 9–10
field theory (FT) 62, 65–68
first zone 85; *see also* model of zones
Flanders, S. 4
framing function 56–57
free associative state 56
Freud, S. 1–8, 17n4, 97; on Aristotle 4, 6, 8, 26, 30n4; on belief in God 103; *Beyond the Pleasure Principle* 6; dreams/dreaming for (*see* dreams/dreaming, Freud's theory of); 'Dreams and Occultism' 42; "The Future of an Illusion" 103; *The Interpretation of Dreams* 1, 3–8, 17n1, 97; "A Metapsychological Supplement to the Theory of Dreams" 6; pleasure principle 29, 52, 85
Fuentes, C. 124
"The Future of an Illusion" (Freud) 103

Gagnebin, M. 104
Garbuz, Y. 81
García Márquez, G. 2
Gasquet, H. 111
Gasquet, J. 109, 111, 115n4
Grayling, A. C. 42
The Great Mystical Circus see Beatriz
Grotstein, J. 1, 10, 16, 17n16; *A Beam of Intense Darkness* 22; "Dreaming as A Curtain of Illusion" 11, 22
Guattari, F. 85

hallucinosis 65
Harris, M. 32
Heraclitus 73, 74
Herrera, H. 120, 122
Hugo, V. 105n4
Hustwit, J. R. 73

ideational reverie 67
illusion 103, 140
infantile wish 4, 5
infinite dimension 23
insight *vs.* intuition 62
International Bion Conference 2–3
International Journal of Psychoanalysis 40

interpretation 79–80
The Interpretation of Dreams (Freud) 1, 3–8, 17n1, 97
intuition 13, 61–68, 78, 79; concept 61; field theory (FT) 62, 65–68; insight *vs.* 62; sixth sense as 95; vitality to analytic process 68; we-ness 13, 63–67
invariance 72, 74, 77
The Italian Seminars (Bion) 95

Jenkins, T. 10
Jewish mystical tradition 13, 74–78
Jimenez, J. P. 6
Johnson, S. 98
Jung, C. G. 7

Kahlo, F. 123–131; abortions 122; bus accident 122, 130, 132n8; *The Bus* (painting) 132n8; death 122, 127; diary writing 123, 131; "las Cachuchas" 122; marriage 123, 126; medical complications 126–127; miscarriages 122, 123; pain 122–123; self-portrait 123, 133n12; sexuality 123–124; as a teenager 122; as a woman with passion 127, 133n16; Zamora on 127
Klein, M. 7, 13, 23, 32–35, 85, 95
Knafo, D. 133n12
knowing 12, 39–48; assertive statements 40; selected fact 47; suffering 43–47
knowing-about 39
Kohut, H. 6

Lacan, J. 59n1, 68
Lahdelma, I. 138
Langton, B. 98
Language and the Schizophrenic (Bion) 47–48
language game 48
Lansky, M. R. 3
Larson, S. 137, 141
latent dream 5, 7, 27
Learning from Experience (Bion) 2, 8, 42
Levine, H. 14, 132n1
Lima, J. 136, 142
listening: to dreams 86; suspicious 64; without memory 62–63
Lobo, E. 16, 136
The Long Week-End 1897–1919 (Bion) 133n17

Mahon, E. 14
Maia, T. 139
Mancia, M. 7, 17n10
manifest dream 5, 6–7, 28; ego 6; Jung on 7; Meltzer on 7
Mann, S. 111
Matte Blanco, I. 84
meaning making 24, 25, 29
Meltzer, D. 16, 7, 32, 70–71, 73, 133n16, 136–137
A Memoir of the Future (Bion) 16, 23, 75, 108, 114, 118–121, 123, 127, 130–131, 133n17; Eigen on 10, 17n14
'Memory and Desire' (Bion) 39
mentation 4, 5
Meregnani, A. 105
Merleau-Ponty, M. 110, 113
"A Metapsychological Supplement to the Theory of Dreams" (Freud) 6
model of zones 84–89
molecular method 6
Monteiro, J. S. 11, 13, 15, 17n12
myths 102, 105n6; personal 100–101; science and 100

Nagel, J. J. 137–138
Nascimento, M. 136
negative capability/faith (NC/F) 62, 65–66

O (at-one-ment) 12, 23, 29, 57, 59, 71, 87
objective meaning 29
Ogden, T. 2, 11–12, 129; *This Art of Psychoanalysis* 17n17; dreaming analytic session 10
Ogilvie, J. 48
omnipotence 103
oneiric dimensions of mind 2, 13–16; aesthetic 124–126; analytic session 90–95; diameter of the circle 71, 72, 75–80; erotic 123–124; family 120–122; finite 126–127; infinite 127–129; model of zones 84–89; pain 122–123; reality 78–81; social 126
Oneiric Dimensions of the Mind (Bion) 2
O'Shaughnessy, E. 42, 114

painting 15; Cézanne's work (*see* Cézanne, P.); coloured touches 110, 111; Kahlo's work (*see* Kahlo, F.)
Parres, R. 127, 133n15
perceptions 4, 56, 85, 86
Phillips, A. 128

Philosophical Investigations (Wittgenstein) 39, 41–42, 47–48
physical mimetism 137
plagal cadence 137, 142
pleasure principle 29, 52, 85
Poincaré, H. 47
Pontalis, J.-B. 1
Popper, K. R. 100
prenatal psyche 128
Process Philosophy 73–74
psychical identity 81
'The Psycho-Analytic Study of Thinking' (Bion) 40
psychotic dreaming 66

rationalism 73
reality 71–81; Jewish mystical tradition 13, 74–78; oneiric dimensions of mind 78–81; Process Philosophy 73–74; in transit 74
reason 85
representation 5; conscious 28; embodied existence 110; ideational 26–27; unconscious 28
reverie 12, 26, 27, 49, 62, 67, 129; analyst 99, 105n3; Bion on 8, 17n11; ideational 67
Rezze, C. J. 127
Rilke, R. M. 113
Rimbaud, A. 62
Rivera, D. 123, 126

Sandler, P. C. 10, 11
Santamaría, J. 1–17
Schiele, E. 133n12
Schneider, J. 11, 12
science 100
second zone 85–88; *see also* model of zones; third zone
Segal, H. 7; theory of symbolism 32, 33–34
selected fact 47
self 23
self-interpreting-through-dreaming 65
self-portraits: Fuentes on 124; Kahlo 123, 124, 133n12; mirror phase 124
self-state dreams 6
sensations 59, 108–112
sensory experience 58–59
sexuality 123–124
shock 68n3
sleep 4
speculation 73, 74

Such Stuff as Dreams (Mahon) 14
suffering 43–47; clinical illustration 43–45; as discovering something 46
suspicious listening 64
symbolism 28; Segal's theory of 32, 33–34

Taming Wild Thoughts (Bion) 123
Tarantelli, C. B. 130, 131
'Theory of Thinking' (Bion) 39, 40, 41
thinking 29–30; speculative 63; unconscious 10
third zone 87–88; *see also* model of zones; second zone
Tractatus Logico-Philosophicus (Wittgenstein) 39, 40, 41
transformation 25, 61; emotional experiences 71–72; invariance and 74, 77
Transformations (Bion) 15, 85, 90, 111, 117, 129
tritones 137–138, 139

ultimate reality of analytic session 71–73
unconscious 1, 4, 9; ego 84; phantasies 86; repressed 50; theoretical preconceptions 62; thinking 10; unstructured 28; *see also* oneiric dimensions of mind
Ur 101–104; *see also* "Death Pit of the Royal Cemetery of Ur"

Vermote, R. 109, 113
Virgil 97, 110, 114
visual images 9–10

"we" vertex (we-ness) 13, 63–67
Whitehead, A. N. 73–74
Williams, M. H. 10, 124, 131, 138, 139
Winnicott, D. W. 32, 34, 35, 51, 54–55
Wittgenstein, L. 39–43, 47–48; *Philosophical Investigations* 39, 41–42, 47–48; *Tractatus* 39, 40, 41; World War One 41
Woolley, C. L. 102, 103

you/I 63

Zamora, M. 120, 127
zones, model of *see* model of zones

For Product Safety Concerns and Information please contact our EU
representative GPSR@taylorandfrancis.com
Taylor & Francis Verlag GmbH, Kaufingerstraße 24, 80331 München, Germany

www.ingramcontent.com/pod-product-compliance
Lightning Source LLC
Chambersburg PA
CBHW070229020526
44113CB00050B/2175